A Supplement to
JESUS CHRIST: FUNDAMENTALS OF CHRISTOLOGY

ROCH KERESZTY, O.Cist.

A Supplement to

JESUS CHRIST:
Fundamentals of Christology

Including
A Reader's Guide and Update
and
St. Bernard's Christology

1997

ALBA·HOUSE   NEW·YORK

SOCIETY OF ST. PAUL, 2187 VICTORY BLVD., STATEN ISLAND, NEW YORK 10314

ST PAULS

Produced and designed in the United States of America by the
Fathers and Brothers of the Society of St. Paul,
2187 Victory Boulevard, Staten Island, New York 10314,
as part of their communications apostolate.

ISBN: 0-8189-0800-9

Printing Information:

Current Printing - first digit	1	2	3	4	5	6	7	8	9	10

Year of Current Printing - first year shown

1997	1998	1999	2000	2001	2002	2003	2004	2005

TABLE OF CONTENTS

Biblical Abbreviations

OLD TESTAMENT

Genesis	Gn	Nehemiah	Ne	Baruch	Ba
Exodus	Ex	Tobit	Tb	Ezekiel	Ezk
Leviticus	Lv	Judith	Jdt	Daniel	Dn
Numbers	Nb	Esther	Est	Hosea	Ho
Deuteronomy	Dt	1 Maccabees	1 M	Joel	Jl
Joshua	Jos	2 Maccabees	2 M	Amos	Am
Judges	Jg	Job	Jb	Obadiah	Ob
Ruth	Rt	Psalms	Ps	Jonah	Jon
1 Samuel	1 S	Proverbs	Pr	Micah	Mi
2 Samuel	2 S	Ecclesiastes	Ec	Nahum	Na
1 Kings	1 K	Song of Songs	Sg	Habakkuk	Hab
2 Kings	2 K	Wisdom	Ws	Zephaniah	Zp
1 Chronicles	1 Ch	Sirach	Si	Haggai	Hg
2 Chronicles	2 Ch	Isaiah	Is	Malachi	Ml
Ezra	Ezr	Jeremiah	Jr	Zechariah	Zc
		Lamentations	Lm		

NEW TESTAMENT

Matthew	Mt	Ephesians	Eph	Hebrews	Heb
Mark	Mk	Philippians	Ph	James	Jm
Luke	Lk	Colossians	Col	1 Peter	1 P
John	Jn	1 Thessalonians	1 Th	2 Peter	2 P
Acts	Ac	2 Thessalonians	2 Th	1 John	1 Jn
Romans	Rm	1 Timothy	1 Tm	2 John	2 Jn
1 Corinthians	1 Cor	2 Timothy	2 Tm	3 John	3 Jn
2 Corinthians	2 Cor	Titus	Tt	Jude	Jude
Galatians	Gal	Philemon	Phm	Revelation	Rv

PREFACE

This supplement was born from the desire to satisfy a number of needs.

1. Surprisingly, my Christology which I had intended for use as a graduate text, attracted a much wider audience. The quick sell out of the first printing, the urgent need for a reprint, and the published and private comments of my critics and readers convinced me that the book is being read not only by graduate students of theology. Priests and lay people remarked that the reading of *Jesus Christ* enriched their spiritual lives and deepened their preaching and teaching. It has also been successfully used for undergraduate courses. The gratitude I feel for being able to help many people of different backgrounds impels me to help them more: I would like to explain to my present and future readers how to use the book selectively, in order to fit their particular needs.

2. The large number of references to primary and secondary sources makes it difficult to sort out what further readings could be most helpful for further research. So I include here a short, selected bibliography for most chapters. Moreover, to help the readers find the highlights of each chapter and facilitate their understanding, I also provide a list of review questions. Some of the questions, especially the ones attached to bibliographical entries, have been designed to stimulate further research which goes beyond the scope of my book.

3. Since I completed the manuscript of *Jesus Christ*,[1] many new books have been published on christological topics, especially concerning the problem of the historical Jesus. Hence, the need

---

[1] From now, referred to as *JC.*

for an update. I had to evaluate these studies and call attention to some of the valuable contributions. In such cases, I suggest that the reader add the text of the *Supplement* to the text of *JC* as indicated in this guide.

4. The repeated teaching of a Christology course since the publication of *JC*, as well as the reading of the reviews and letters of my critics, has helped me clarify some of my presuppositions and correct or better articulate some of my conclusions. In these instances I suggest that the reader replace the pages in *JC* with the new text as indicated in the *Supplement*.

5. Sara Butler, the most thorough reviewer of *JC*,[2] noticed the deep impact that St. Bernard's existential correlation of anthropology and Christology had on my work. In fact, if the reader has appreciated my Christology, he or she will appreciate even more that of Bernard. As a last part of the *Supplement*, then, a longer study of mine, "Relationship between Anthropology and Christology: St. Bernard, a Teacher for Our Age" will be reprinted from a European journal. May its reading promote the discovery of one of the greatest forgotten treasures in our theological tradition!

6. Finally, one general clarification and an apology are in order. My mother tongue is Hungarian, which does not need to struggle with developing inclusive language for the simple reason that it has never used anything else. The same personal pronoun serves for "he" and "she," and two different nouns mean "human being" and "male human being" respectively. Thus, my use of "he" for a general pronoun is due to my struggle to find the simplest way of expressing myself in the standard English I have learned; it is not meant as an ideological stance to ignore, let alone hurt, feminine sensitivities. In an eventual revised edition I intend to use horizontal inclusive language to the best of my linguistic abilities.

---

[2] "*Jesus Christ: Fundamentals of Christology*: An appreciation," *Communio* 23 (1996) 419-426.

How to Use the Book for Different Purposes

If you use *JC* as a graduate text, the ideal framework would be two, semester-long three credit courses. Traditionally, schools divide the material into two courses, Christology in the strict sense, and Soteriology, whereas *JC* shows the inseparable connection between these two aspects of the mystery of Christ. Thus, my recommendation is to divide the two semesters between historical and systematic Christology (Christology in the broad sense of including both the person and work of Christ). Under such optimal conditions you can fully utilize the footnotes which conduct a condensed dialogue with other historians and contemporary systematic theologians. You can also study some of the recommended readings, treat some biblical themes, individual theologians or particular aspects of the mystery of Christ more in depth. If you must condense all the material into one semester, an intelligent selection process will be needed, unless the class is extremely bright and well prepared. You can drop most of the footnote texts, even some chapters of the historical Christology. For an undergraduate Christology course you could omit the entire historical part after Luther and Calvin.

If you were to use the book for an apologetics course, I recommend that you select chapters I, II, IV & V of Part I as well as Appendix I, concentrating on the method of historiography, the death and Resurrection of Jesus, the implicit Christology of the "historical Jesus" and his uniqueness in the history of religions. Of course, for theodicy and for showing the necessity and role of the Church in mediating faith, other works should also be used. In general, I found that the best apologetics is not an endless discussion with opponents (even though contemporary difficulties to Christian faith must be taken seriously) but rather a peaceful exposition of the full mystery of Christ. This should be done in such a way that the unique form of God's love manifested in Christ may become perceptible to those who are searching for pure love. The best apologetics is indeed the study of Christology in its integrity.

For personal enrichment, any part of the book can be read selectively; for spiritual reading I recommend most of the biblical part, the soteriology of the Fathers, St. Bernard, K. Barth, D. Bonhoeffer and most of the systematic part.

Following closely the structure of *JC* (parts & chapters), three items are featured in the *Reader's Guide and Update:*

1. Some chapters begin with clarifications and corrections or the discussion of new insights or literature on the subject. Certain texts replace a few pages in *Jesus Christ,* others are additions to the original text.

2. Under the title, *Recommended Readings,* the reader will find a highly selective list of works which are essential for further orientation on the topic under discussion. The selected works present positions either close or opposed to varying degrees to my Christology. Whereas I was able to add to or elaborate on just a few chapters, recommended readings are assigned to most chapters. The order of recommended works follows the topical sequence within a chapter and their perceived importance within the same topic.

3. Finally, a list of study questions to pinpoint important issues, check understanding and help organize the reader's thoughts is appended to each chapter.

PART I
CHRISTOLOGY OF THE NEW TESTAMENT

INTRODUCTION

Recommended Readings

The following important works provide different approaches to Christology in general.

W. Kasper, *Jesus the Christ* (New York: Paulist, 1977). Although somewhat dated and poorly translated, Kasper's book remains a valuable synthesis. It integrates modern biblical scholarship and philosophy into the classic christological tradition. Its typically German perspective, however, creates difficulties for the average American reader. In order to locate the mystery of Christ in its Trinitarian context, the book should be complemented by parts of Kasper's most mature theological synthesis, *The God of Jesus Christ* (New York: Crossroad, 1984).

Hans Urs von Balthasar, *The Glory of the Lord: A Theological Aesthetics,* vols. I-VII, *Theo-Drama,* vols. I-IV (San Francisco: Ignatius Press, 1985-94 (publication of *Theo-Logic,* vols. I-III is planned for the immediate future). This immense trilogy is a most impressive contemporary theological synthesis centered on Christ. It shows how the splendor of God's love manifested in Christ (theological aesthetics) is the one fully credible evidence of revelation. This love reveals its ultimate depth in the drama of Salvation History played out between finite human and infinite divine freedoms. The theo-drama reaches its climax in the mystery of the cross. Finally, the implications of the truth of divine love are investigated in what is called "theo-logic." While rich in insights, this monumental work is often repetitious. Its greatest attraction for our contemporaries lies in its fundamental intuition: The unfolding mystery of Christ is God's response to the human yearning for pure, infinite love implicit in any genuine interpersonal relationship (cf. "Meeting God in Today's World," *Concilium,* vol. 6, pp. 23-39).

1

Balthasar's interpretation of Jesus' descent to hell as a temporary suffering of hell (based not on patristic tradition but on Barthian theology and the mystic visions of Adrienne von Speyr), a descent that makes after-death conversions possible, seems to me the most questionable aspect of his Christology.

K. Rahner, *The Foundations of Christian Faith* (New York: Crossroad, 1978). While more comprehensive than a Christology, it provides a synthesis of Rahner's christological vision with references to his articles for a more detailed treatment of particular themes. I have profited much from his insights, especially regarding the openness of human nature toward God and the relationship between created and uncreated freedom.

However, we need to investigate further Rahner's understanding of the relationship between transcendental and historical Christology. Does he not try to deduce too much from the *a priori* conditions of God's absolute gift of self for the concrete shape of the Jesus event?

Moreover, it should also be researched to what extent Rahner's understanding of Trinitarian personhood as "mode of subsistence" (*Subsistenzweise*) jeopardizes the understanding of the personal, dialogical character of God's Trinitarian life. Does Rahner not end up with a divine-human partnership exemplified in Jesus Christ and participated in to varying degrees by other human beings, instead of seeing the goal of redemption as humankind's assumption into the eternal life of Trinitarian communion? Has Rahner's silence over God as personal communion of Three Divine Persons not led to the development of "Catholic" process theologies, a development that Rahner himself had rightly opposed?

G. O'Collins, *Christology: A Biblical, Historical, and Systematic Study of Jesus* (New York: Oxford University Press, 1995) is the most recent Catholic Christology. O'Collins intends to remain faithful to the Catholic tradition while showing sensitivity to contemporary concerns. In general, he is balanced and helpful, but his treatment of biblical, patristic, and systematic Soteriology remains incomplete.

J. Macquarrie, *Jesus Christ in Modern Thought* (Philadelphia: Trinity Press International, 1990). It treats not only modern Christologies, but provides an intelligent historical survey beginning with Christ in the New Testament. Its lucid summaries of modern Christologies, both Protestant and Catholic, are especially valuable. Yet, Macquarrie's own Christology, in spite of the author's intention, does not do justice to the essential claims of Christian faith. For instance, how can a Christian theologian provide two alternative endings to the story of Jesus: "the happy ending" that affirms Resurrection and Ascension, and the "austere ending" in which Jesus has not been raised from the dead?

Study Questions

1. What is the one major presupposition for the shape and content of the book *Jesus Christ?*
2. What are the implications of this one major presupposition?
3. What is the role of the New Testament witness to Christ in relation to the Old Testament?
4. What is the role of the New Testament regarding future christological developments?
5. What is the role of the Magisterium regarding future christological developments?
6. On what grounds do we affirm that we can find valuable christological insights in the work of non-Catholic Christian theologians?
7. On what grounds do we affirm that we can find new perspectives for understanding the mystery of Christ in non-Christian religions?

CHAPTER I — THE METHOD OF BIBLICAL CHRISTOLOGY

New Text
(Add to the end of 1. *Critique of the "Liberal Quest" and of the "New Quest for the Historical Jesus,"* p. 8).

While the more modest, second quest continues to produce

works of valuable scholarship[3] (even if some of its presuppositions and conclusions call for a critical review), something radically new came on the scene in the 90's: skillfully, a small number of scholars began to take advantage of the media's insatiable craving for shocking novelties. They started to produce one extravagant "historical reconstruction" of the historical Jesus after another, and to increase the influence of their works, they provided a series of interviews for the media. One of the most important first books of this trend was produced by J.D. Crossan, *The Historical Jesus: The Life of a Mediterranean Jewish Peasant*.[4] This new trend, which we may call the "Third Quest," has continued with the work of the "Jesus Seminar" and the books published by its members. But the novelty of this trend hardly goes beyond its skillful art of media manipulation. It produced a new mutant of the old virus which had infected the Liberal Quest of the 19th century: the unexamined ideological commitments of the writer predetermine his conclusions. As a result, Jesus, the cynic sage, Jesus, the anti-cultural hero of the politics of compassion, and Jesus, Lady Sophia's prophet, all became the predictable projections of their authors' social agenda.[5] Just as the Liberal Quest of the 19th century, the authors we identified as belonging to the "Third Quest" all agree that their

---

[3] One of its most important contributions concerns only indirectly, but quite decisively, the starting point of the historical Jesus research: J. Fitzmyer has produced convincing evidence for the traditional position that Luke was indeed a contemporary and companion to Paul. This fact reestablishes the Acts' basic historical credibility and provides evidence in support of the New Testament view of Christian origins. See J. Fitzmyer, *Luke the Theologian: Aspects of His Teaching* (NY: Paulist, 1989), pp. 1-27.

[4] New York: Harper San Francisco, 1991.

[5] See for instance, M.J. Borg, *Jesus: A New Vision: Spirit, Culture and the Life of Discipleship* (San Francisco: Harper SF, 1991); —*Meeting Jesus Again for the First Time: The Historical Jesus and the Heart of Contemporary Faith* (San Francisco: Harper SF, 1994); *Five Gospels: The Search for the Authentic Words of Jesus*, intr. & tr. by R.W. Funk & R.W. Hoover (New York: Macmillan, 1993); B. Mack, *The Lost Gospel: The Book of Q and Christian Origins* (San Francisco: Harper SF, 1993); E. Schussler Fiorenza, *In Memory of Her* (New York: Crossroad, 1983). All these works assume that later Church authorities suppressed or truncated the most authentic forms of the Jesus tradition while the New Testament canon is the result of their successful grab for power. Consequently, the apocryphal gospels, in particular, the Gospel of Thomas, the Secret Gospel of Mark, the Gospel of Peter are more reliable sources for them than the canonical gospels. Within the canon the so-called Q document (hypothesized to have existed as a separate

own reconstruction of the historical Jesus is the only real Jesus accessible to our age and thus it must replace the Church's traditional Christ of faith. As Crossan puts it, "If you cannot believe in something produced by reconstruction, you may have nothing left to believe in."[6]

No wonder that this "Third Quest" soon generated a new skepticism regarding the ability of the historian *qua* historian to grasp in any way the "real Jesus." The pendulum seems to be swinging back again to a position similar to where it was after Schweitzer and before Käsemann. This skepticism regarding historical studies spread not only among ordinary Christians but also among those biblical scholars who take seriously their Christian faith commitment. Some of them decided against venturing into any "new rethinking" of the so-called historical Jesus and chose to accept directly, without any mediation of historical criticism, the full apostolic witness to Jesus as has been presented by the New Testament and unfolded by the Church's tradition.[7] Others resolved to refrain from studying the historical reliability of the Gospels and restrict themselves to a mere literary analysis which studies the Gospels as unified compositions.

The question, then, arises with a new urgency: Is it still possible to use a critically reviewed historical-critical method to reconstruct at least a fragment of the real Jesus, and if so, how can we move from there to the full portrait of Jesus as presented by the whole of the New Testament? In the section of *JC* on the method

---

document because of the material common to Mt and Lk not found in Mk) is their preferred source (even though such a document has never been found and its existence is increasingly questioned by a growing number of scholars). Even though L.T. Johnson is unfairly skeptical regarding any reconstruction of the "historical Jesus," he provides a brilliant critique of the above mentioned scholars: L.T. Johnson, *The Real Jesus. The Misguided Quest for the Historical Jesus and the Truth of the Traditional Gospels* (San Francisco: Harper SF, 1996) pp. 1-104.

[6] *The Historical Jesus*, p. 426.

[7] For instance, Luke T. Johnson, *The Real Jesus* (see footnote #5) and William M. Thompson, *The Struggle for Theology's Soul: Contesting Scripture in Christology* (New York: Crossroad, 1996). Even though Thompson does not provide a critical foundation for his method, his integration of the full New Testament witness to Christ with the tradition of the Church marks an important turning point in the history of contemporary mainstream American Catholic theology.

of biblical Christology (pp. 8-20), and in two articles published afterwards, I attempt to outline an answer.[8]

Recommended Readings

Some of the most responsible works which are, to varying degrees, successful in reconstructing a "Jesus of History" are as follows:

B.F. Meyer, "Jesus Christ," *Anchor Bible Dictionary,* vol. 3 (New York: Doubleday, 1992), 773-796. It seems to me the best short summary of what a historian as historian can say about Jesus.

X. Léon-Dufour, *The Gospels and the Jesus of History* (New York: Desclée, 1967). Although somewhat dated, it is still a more plausible reconstruction than many contemporary attempts.

J.H. Charlesworth, *Jesus within Judaism. New Light from Exciting Archaeological Discoveries* (New York: Doubleday, 1988). It locates Jesus within contemporary Judaism and provides a detailed bibliography on the "historical Jesus" research.

J.P. Meier, *A Marginal Jew: Rethinking the Historical Jesus,* vols. I & II (New York: Doubleday, 1991-4). A third volume is in the making. The first two volumes contain a treasury of vast knowledge and an impressive command of primary and secondary literature. Yet, in spite of the immense erudition, the conclusions at times come close to platitudes; the work does not sufficiently grasp what is unique in the Jesus phenomenon.

L.T. Johnson, *The Real Jesus. The Misguided Quest for the Historical Jesus and the Truth of the Traditional Gospels* (New York: Harper San Francisco, 1996). It is a brilliant critique of the latest phase in the "historical Jesus" research, but unduly restrictive about the scope of historical research in general.

---

[8] R. Kereszty, "Historical Research, Theological Inquiry, and the Reality of Jesus: Reflections on the Method of J.P. Meier," *Communio* 19 (1992) 575-600; — "The Role of the 'Jesus of History' Research within the Theological Enterprise" to be published in the second issue of *Communio* in 1997. In fact, the above text is a modified version of this second article.

Study Questions

1. What is the basic presupposition of the Liberal Quest for the historical Jesus?
2. What causes put an end to the Liberal Quest?
3. When and how did the New Quest begin? Why?
4. Explain the inadequacies of the New Quest.
5. What characterizes the "Third Quest" which emerged in the early nineties? To what extent is it justifiable to say that the quest for the historical Jesus moves in cycles?
6. Define the basic presuppositions of the method of the biblical part of this book. In particular:
   a) Show how "facts" are the product of objective data and interpretation.
   b) Show why a historian, *pace* L.T. Johnson, must go beyond facts.
   c) In order to understand the history of a person or persons, what else is needed beyond a knowledge of data and a rational analysis of the data? Why are the latter not sufficient?
   d) Why should a historian resist the rationalistic attempt at subsuming every new act and person under general categories?
   e) Why can every human person be understood only from the perspective of his death?
   f) Why and how does the question of meaning arise in the study of history?
   g) How does the question of the meaning of history call for a philosophy or theology of history?
   h) In the light of what has been said above, how does the method of historiography and the question of meaning in history call for a theological history of Jesus?
   i) What can such a theological history of Jesus accomplish? What are its limitations?
7. What is assured by the inspiration of the biblical documents concerning Jesus?
8. What is not assured by inspiration? (For the answers to these last two questions see also *Dei Verbum*, n. 11.)

9. How is the historical uncertainty about some events and sayings of Jesus consistent with the reality of the Incarnation?
10. How can you prove the general historicity of the New Testament records about Jesus?
11. Explain each criterion for an authentic Jesus tradition. Give examples for each.
12. What is the value of a partial reconstruction by biblical scholars of the reality of Jesus (the construct: "historical Jesus") for apologetics? Besides this chapter consult also pp. 50-51, 108-117 for a full answer.

CHAPTER II — THE DEATH AND RESURRECTION OF JESUS

Recommended Readings

D. Kendall, G. O'Collins, "The Uniqueness of the Easter Appearances," *CBQ* 54 (1992), 287-307. This thorough study concludes that the appearances of the risen Christ as reported in the New Testament are restricted with regard to time and persons. They belong to the foundational stage of the Church and therefore they were given only to a chosen group of witnesses. Their nature is different from later ecstatic experiences, verbal communications of Christ, and manifestations of the Holy Spirit that have continued in the history of the Church.

G. O'Collins, *Interpreting the Resurrection* (New York: Paulist, 1988). A balanced study, informative of contemporary opinions.

R. Brown, *The Virginal Conception and Bodily Resurrection of Jesus* (New York: Paulist, 1973). Even today, the part on the Resurrection remains one of the best studies on the subject.

Study Questions

1. What are the advantages of starting biblical Christology with an analysis of the proclamation of Jesus' saving death and Resurrection by his disciples?
2. How can you prove the historicity of Jesus' death on the cross?
3. Give the logical steps of the book's argument which concludes that it is reasonable to believe in the bodily Resurrection of Jesus.
4. Give a detailed exegesis of I Cor 15:3-8. (In particular, why is this text so important for our purpose? How old is the tradition embodied in 3b-5? Does Paul view the appearance of Jesus to himself as a historical event? If so, what special kind?)
5. Interpret the appearance narratives of both the Gospels and Acts, as well as the empty tomb narratives.
6. What facts connected with the origin of Resurrection faith can be established by the historian? In particular, how do you prove the historicity of the empty tomb?
7. Explain the theories which deny any form of Resurrection.
8. Explain the various interpretations of the Resurrection of Christ.
9. Interpret the epistemological status of the appearances of Jesus:
   a) What extreme interpretations should be excluded?
   b) What does it mean that the appearances were revelatory signs of the risen Christ?
   c) In order to recognize an appearance of the risen Christ, what else did the disciples need beside sense perception? Why was sense perception not sufficient to recognize the identity of the risen Lord?
   d) Were the appearances historical events? Explain.
   e) How are the appearances related to the sacraments?
   f) How does the fact of the empty tomb contribute to our understanding of the reality of the risen Christ?
10. How can history, philosophy, and theology contribute to the credibility of the Resurrection of Jesus?

CHAPTER III — THE BEGINNING OF THE GOSPEL

New Text
(Replace the first 16 lines on p. 59 with the following text)

Since the publication of *JC* some very interesting new research has been published concerning the question of the brothers and sisters of Jesus. Ironically, the most effective challenge to the view of the Catholic biblical scholar J.P. Meier came from a Protestant historian, W. Bauckham.[9] According to Meier, prescinding from faith and later Church teaching, the most probable conclusion of the historian cannot be anything else but that "the brothers and sisters of Jesus were true siblings."[10] Bauckham, however, finds considerable new evidence in favor of the long dismissed fourth-century view of Epiphanius, according to whom the "brothers and sisters of Jesus" come from a first marriage of Joseph, and thus, Jesus is the only son of Mary. Bauckham's position is all the more noteworthy since he has no doctrinal investment in Mary's perpetual virginity; in fact he is convinced that after Jesus' birth Mary and Joseph had normal sexual relations. The most important arguments of Bauckham are as follows:

1. The brothers and sisters of Jesus appear older than Jesus in all Gospel traditions whereas Jesus is clearly affirmed to have been the firstborn son of Mary. Younger brothers in Jewish society at that time could hardly have assumed the authority over the firstborn son that is attributed to the "brothers and sisters of Jesus" by the Gospels: they try to advise him (Jn 7:3-5); they want to stop him in his ministry (Mk 3:21, 31).

2. Second century apocryphal writings such as the Protoevangelium of James, the Infancy Gospel of Thomas and the Gospel of Peter (literarily independent from each other) take for granted that the brothers and sisters of Jesus come from Joseph's previous marriage "as something the readers already know to be

---

[9] "The Brothers and Sisters of Jesus: An Epiphanian Response to J.P. Meier" *CBQ* 56 (1994), 686-700.

[10] "The Brothers and Sisters of Jesus in Ecumenical Perspective" *CBQ* 54 (1992), 26.

the case." Bauckham, of course, is aware that these apocryphal documents are the conflation of tradition and creative imagination. Yet, he points out that the above datum is not their creation (How could they create the same story independently from each other?) but a common tradition in (probably early) second-century Syrian Christianity which evidently predates all three documents and may well go back to the oral Gospel of the church of Antioch.[11]

3. It is a well known fact that the Gospel of Mark never refers to Jesus as "son of Joseph," but only as "son of Mary." Up to now, no one was able to come up with an entirely plausible solution for this divergence from Jewish custom which would normally require the identification of the son by the father's name. Bauckham thinks that "in Nazareth Jesus would have been known as 'the son of Mary' because this distinguished him from the children of Joseph by his first wife." He lists a long series of parallels for this usage from the Old Testament.[12]

Bauckham has indeed successfully demonstrated that Meier's method is quite questionable and that he has neglected some important evidence in favor of the Epiphanian view. Thus, the historical question remains much more open than Meier has suggested.

For Bauckham the whole issue is merely a question of historical method and an interesting piece of historical trivia without any theological consequences. For Catholic theologians, however, it better explains why the Church was able to hold on simultaneously to the tradition of Jesus' "brothers and sisters" while, at the same time, develop the teaching on Mary's perpetual virginity.

Recommended Readings

W. Bauckham, "The Brothers and Sisters of Jesus: An Epiphanian Response to J.P. Meier," *CBQ* 56 (1994), 686-700. See comments above.

---

[11] Bauckham, 696-697.

[12] Bauckham, 699-700.

R. Brown, *The Birth of the Messiah: A Commentary on the Infancy Narratives in Matthew and Luke,* Revised ed. *Anchor Bible Reference Library* (Garden City: Doubleday, 1993). A wealth of information, but in theological depth and refinement the book is no match to

R. Laurentin, *Structure et théologie de Luc I-II* (Paris: Gabalda, 1957); *Jésus au Temple. Mystère de Pâques et foi de Marie en Luc 2,48-50* (Paris: Gabalda, 1966). Unfortunately, neither of these books has been translated into English.

Study Questions

1. Explain the analogy between the mystery of Jesus' virginal conception and the mystery of his Resurrection.
2. How can you show that the tradition of the virginal conception of Jesus does not derive from Hellenistic religions?
3. How is the mystery of the virginal conception prepared in the Old Testament?
4. What is the theological meaning of Jesus' virginal conception? What is common to both Mt and Lk, what is special to Mt and what is special to Lk?
5. What can be shown historically about the fact of the virginal conception?
6. How is faith related to what is historically demonstrable? (Show the analogy between the fact of the empty tomb and the early pregnancy of Mary.)
7. What can and cannot be proved from the New Testament concerning the "brothers and sisters of Jesus"?
8. What arguments does Bauckham present in favor of the Epiphanian view regarding "the brothers and sisters of Jesus"?
9. How did Church tradition develop regarding the perpetual virginity of Mary?
10. How is the perpetual virginity of Mary connected with the mystery of her universal motherhood?
11. How is the mystery of Mary's perpetual virginity related to the mystery of the Church?

12. How does the mystery of the Holy Family shed light on the mystery of religious communities, ecclesial communities, and Christian marriage?
13. According to the New Testament Jesus is the "Son of David." What historical evidence do we have for the Davidic descent of Jesus? What is the theological meaning of this title?
14. Compare the story of the twelve-year-old Jesus in the Temple with the call of Samuel (I Sam 2:19-26). What are the similarities and differences?
15. Comment on the theological meaning of Jesus' "private life" before his public ministry.

CHAPTER IV — JESUS AND THE KINGDOM

From among an immense body of literature I selected two outstanding treatments of the theme "Kingdom of God":

B.F. Meyer, *The Aims of Jesus* (London: SCM Press, 1979), pp. 111-253.

W. Kasper, *Jesus the Christ*, pp. 72-88.

R. Latourelle, *The Miracles of Jesus and the Theology of Miracles* (New York: Paulist, 1988). This work is informative and helpful regarding the historicity of Jesus' miracles and their meaning.

I. de la Potterie, "The Multiplication of the Loaves in the Life of Jesus," *Communio* 16 (1989), 499-516. This small article is a masterpiece which shows how to use and transcend the historical critical method in interpreting the fact and the meaning of the multiplication of the loaves.

Study Questions

1. How can you "prove" the historicity of the baptism of Jesus by John?
2. Explain the message of John.
3. How is Jesus' message opposed to that of John? Yet, how is

the good news of Jesus related to the preaching of divine judgment by John?

4. Explain the meaning of Jesus' baptism by John as a prophetic sign action. How is this sign action better understood in the light of the Resurrection?

5. Explain the meaning of the words of the Father to Jesus at his baptism?

6. Show that the temptation accounts go back, in some form, to a genuine experience of Jesus.

7. How could Jesus be *really* tempted?

8. How does Jesus re-live the temptations of Israel according to Mt?

9. How are the temptations of Jesus universal human temptations according to Lk?

10. How are the temptations of Jesus temptations for the Church in every age?

11. Give a probable outline of the public ministry of Jesus.

12. What is the meaning of the verb *euaggelizesthai,* "proclaim the good news," in the light of its Old Testament usage?

13. What does Jesus mean by the Kingdom of God? How is his understanding of the Kingdom different from that of his contemporaries?

14. Explain the meaning of the central image of the Kingdom.

15. Explain the meaning of *metanoia* in Jesus' preaching. How is it connected with the theme of the Kingdom?

16. Why do the poor, the lame, and the blind have a special advantage regarding the Kingdom?

17. What do the miracles of Jesus say about the Kingdom? What further light do they receive from the Resurrection of Jesus?

18. What evidence do we have for the historicity of Jesus' miracles in general?

19. How is the multiplication of the loaves a turning point in the ministry of Jesus? Explain the evidence for its historicity and the meaning of this sign.

CHAPTER V — THE KINGDOM AND THE DEATH OF JESUS

Recommended Readings

B.F. Meyer, "The Expiation Motif in the Eucharistic Words: A Key to the History of Jesus?" *One Loaf, One Cup. Ecumenical Studies of I Cor 11 and Other Eucharistic Texts* (Macon: Mercer, 1993), pp. 11-33. Perhaps the author wants to prove too much by the historical method, yet his fundamental insight on Jesus' intentions facing death is well established.

R. Brown, *The Death of the Messiah. From Gethsemane to the Grave. A Commentary on the Passion Narratives in the Four Gospels*, vols. I-II. *The Anchor Bible Reference Library* (New York: Doubleday, 1994). Even if it is often too anxious to cling to a consensus on issues of historicity and is somewhat pedestrian in theological interpretation, no one can ignore the immense wealth of the well digested information that these two volumes provide.

I. de la Potterie, *The Hour of Jesus. The Passion and Resurrection of Jesus According to John* (New York: Alba House, 1990). A penetrating theological analysis of the Johannine accounts.

J. Jeremias, *The Prayers of Jesus* (Philadelphia: Fortress, 1978). In spite of some minor modifications by recent scholarship, this is still a respected classic on Jesus' relationship to the Father.

Study Questions

1. How can you show that Jesus saw his death as part of God's plan of salvation?
2. How do the words of Jesus at the Last Supper (Mk 14:22-25) and his actions at this Supper shed light on Jesus' understanding of his own death?
3. Show that Jesus' death as an expiating sacrifice is not opposed to his initial announcement of freely offered forgiveness.
4. What indications do we have for the authenticity of Jesus' cry on the cross, "My God, my God, why have you forsaken me?"

5. What indicates that Jesus predicted his Resurrection? Yet, if he did, how could he truly suffer anguish?
6. Do Mk 9:1, Mt 16:28, Mk 13:30 and Mt 24:34 necessarily imply a chronologically imminent end of the world? Explain.
7. What is Jesus' position on the "day and hour" of the end?
8. How has the Kingdom become present in our world through the death and Resurrection of Jesus? What is still to be expected? Why do we pray every day for its coming?
9. Why could the earthly Jesus have only an implicit Christology?
10. Explain in detail the implicit Christology of Jesus.

CHAPTER VI — THE UNDERSTANDING OF THE MYSTERY OF CHRIST IN THE APOSTOLIC CHURCH

Recommended Readings

C.H. Dodd, *According to the Scriptures. The Substructure of New Testament Theology* (Collins, Fontana Books: 1965). Even today it is an indispensable classic.

R.E. Brown, *An Introduction to New Testament Christology* (New York: Paulist, 1994). One may not always agree with Brown's position; yet, no one can ignore this introduction to the present state of moderate biblical scholarship on New Testament Christology.

M. Hengel, *The Son of God. The Origin of Christology and the History of Jewish-Hellenistic Religion* (Philadelphia: Fortress, 1976). This remains one of the best studies on the origins of New Testament Christology.

A. Feuillet, *The Priesthood of Christ and His Ministers* (Garden City: Doubleday, 1975). The author shows convincingly that, in spite of only one explicit treatment of Jesus' priesthood in the Letter to the Hebrews, the notion of sacrifice is central to a New Testament understanding of redemption.

O. Cullmann, *The Christology of the New Testament* (Philadelphia: Westminster, 1963). Even though the work is dated and the

author sets up an arbitrary opposition between functional and ontological Christology, many of his exegetical insights remain un-
surpassed.

Study Questions

1. How does 1 Peter 1:10-12 interpret christologically the
   whole of the Old Testament?
2. Show that the Suffering Servant passages, combined with
   the Son of Man texts, are the key to a christological interpretation of the Old Testament.
3. Interpret the four Suffering Servant songs in Deutero-
   Isaiah.
4. Explain:
   a) Jesus as the Son of Man
   b) Jesus as the New, Eschatological Israel
   c) Jesus as High Priest and Perfect Sacrifice
   d) Jesus as Messiah
   e) Jesus as Son of Adam and the Last Adam
   f) Jesus as the final and complete theophany of God
      (especially the absolute "I AM" statements in Jn).
5. What is irreducibly new in the New Testament in relation
   to the Old?
6. Explain the early Aramaic origin and the meaning of the
   most ancient confession of faith: "Jesus is Lord."
7. What is the relevance of Jesus' lordship: (a) regarding the
   Eucharist, (b) regarding the Christians' social status and
   relationships, (c) their relationship to the emperor?
8. Explain the meaning of the affirmation: "Jesus is the Son of
   God." In particular, (a) does Jesus call himself "Son of
   God"? (b) what are the sources for the Church's proclamation, "Jesus is the Son of God"? (c) Explain the theology of
   the "Son of God" in Paul, Mk, and Jn.
9. Why is the Church so slow in attributing the title "God" to
   Jesus?
10. Show the central importance of the affirmation that Jesus
    is God in the Gospel of John.
11. Once the divinity of Jesus is clearly expressed conceptually,
    how does it shed new light on the work of our redemption?

PART II
HISTORICAL CHRISTOLOGY

INTRODUCTION TO PATRISTIC CHRISTOLOGY

Recommended Readings

Obviously, the most important readings in the history of Christology are the primary sources, if at all possible in the original language. Given the variety of sources and the many available translations, I entrust their selection to the instructor or reader.

H. de Lubac, "The Pagan Religions and the Fathers of the Church," *The Church: Paradox and Mystery* (New York: Alba House, 1969). The most penetrating survey of the Fathers' understanding of the relationship between Christianity and non-Christian religions and religious philosophies.

Study Questions

1. Explain the method of patristic theology.
2. Explain the relevance of patristic Christology and Soteriology for our age.
3. Why, according to the Fathers, can the word "religion" not be univocally applied to Christianity and to other religions?
4. What considerations ground the unique dignity of Christianity according to the Fathers?
5. Explain the two-way relationship between Christianity and other religions and religious philosophies, according to the Fathers.

CHAPTER I — THE SOTERIOLOGY OF THE FATHERS

Recommended Readings

B. Studer, *Trinity and Incarnation: The Faith of the Early Church* (Collegeville: Liturgical Press, 1993). A precise, reliable work on Trinitarian Theology, Christology and Soteriology.

H.E.W. Turner, *The Patristic Doctrine of Redemption* (London,

Mowbray, 1952). In spite of its age, it is still a worthwhile reading.
R.J. Daly, *Christian Sacrifice. The Judeo-Christian Background before Origen* (Washington: CUA Press, 1978). *The Origins of the Christian Doctrine of Sacrifice* (Philadelphia: Fortress, 1978). These two works are the best available studies in English on this theme.

Study Questions

1. Why is patristic Soteriology treated before patristic Christology in *JC*?
2. Explain the dimensions of sin according to the Fathers.
3. Explain the metaphysical foundation of patristic Soteriology.
4. Explain the following soteriological themes:
    a) Christ as mediator,
    b) the descent and ascent of Christ,
    c) all the dimensions (metaphysical, existential and emotional) of the *admirabile commercium* (marvelous exchange),
    d) redemption as victory and deliverance.
5. Explain the doctrine of Augustine on sacrifice; show the connection between the following themes:
    a) the whole person being a sacrifice,
    b) the Old Testament sacrifices,
    c) the Eucharist,
    d) the sacrifice of Christ.
6. How does the doctrine of the Fathers on Christ as our teacher and example differ from the rationalist Christologies of liberal Protestantism?
7. Explain the christological implication of what Gregory the Great defined in these terms: *amor ipse notitia est* ("love itself is knowledge")?
8. What are the results of sin on the material universe according to the Fathers?
9. Explain the role of Christ regarding the unity of the whole of creation according to Maximus Confessor.
10. Explain how all the above soteriological themes find a unifying center in the notion of communion.

CHAPTER II — THE CHRISTOLOGY OF THE FATHERS

Recommended Readings

A. Grillmeier, *Christ in Christian Tradition*, vols. I-II (Atlanta: J. Knox, 1975-87). This is the best available in-depth history of patristic Christology.

W. Kasper, "'One of the Trinity'...: Reestablishing a Spiritual Christology in the Perspective of Trinitarian Theology," *Theology and Church* (New York: Crossroad, 1989), pp. 94-108. This important article shows that the intent of the Council Fathers at Chalcedon was not to present the whole mystery of Christ in their christological document but to provide a clarification of an article in the Nicene-Constantinopolitan creed. Moreover, Kasper demonstrates that, according to Chalcedon, the ultimate subject of the incarnate Word is the Second Person of the Trinity.

J. Meyendorff, *Christ in Eastern Christian Thought* (Washington: Corpus Publications, 1969). This work is indispensable for learning the Orthodox perspective on the history of Christology.

Study Questions

1. Sketch out the stages of the development of patristic Christology up to the Third Council of Constantinople. (Remember the most important dates: 325, 431, 433, 451, 553, 680-681.)
2. How does St. Ignatius of Antioch react against gnosticism?
3. How is docetism part of the theological climate today?
4. Explain how the Fathers criticized and changed gnosticism into an authentic Christian theology and spirituality.
5. Explain the adoptionism of Paul of Samosata.
6. How does an adoptionist tendency manifest itself today in some Christologies?
7. Explain Arianism as a Hellenistic distortion of Christianity.
8. How does Gregory of Nazianzus argue against Apollinarianism?

9. Explain Gregory of Nazianzus's text which anticipates so well the Chalcedonian definition (*Letter 101, I to Cledonius*, 20-21).

10. How does Tertullian's dialogical understanding of "*persona*" pave the way for a more precise formulation of the Trinitarian and christological mysteries?

11. Explain Augustine's doctrine on the person of Christ.

12. Explain the prevailing terminology as well as the strengths and weaknesses of Alexandrian Christology.

13. Explain the prevailing terminology of Antiochene Christology. (What is one and what is two in Christ, how is the union of the human and divine expressed?)

14. What can the Antiochene school not explain satisfactorily regarding the metaphysical constitution of Christ?

15. What are the strengths of Antiochene Christology?

16. Define the *communicatio idomatum*. What are its basic rules?

17. Why did the Nestorians have problems with the *communicatio idiomatum*?

18. What are the logical consequences of the Nestorian position regarding the motherhood of Mary and our redemption?

19. Summarize the doctrine of the Council of Ephesus on Christ. What questions did the Council not answer?

20. Explain the progress made in the formula of union between John of Antioch and Cyril of Alexandria in 433.

21. Explain the monophysite heresy.

22. Why is it important that the Chalcedonian decree on Christ is not a new creed but a commentary on one of the articles of the Creed? What happened to Christology when this simple fact was forgotten?

23. What new meaning did the word "hypostasis" receive in the Chalcedonian decree?

24. What is new in the Chalcedonian decree in comparison to previous conciliar texts on Christ?

25. Show that monophysitism is an uncritical acceptance of some Hellenistic philosophical principles.

26. What genuine christological truth did the monophysites distort into a Hellenistic doctrine?

3

27. What is new regarding the teaching on Christ in the
document of the Third Council of Constantinople? How is
it rooted in the New Testament? How does the Council's
teaching avoid "splitting Christ" into two subjects?

CHAPTER III — MEDIEVAL CHRISTOLOGY

Recommended Readings

R. Kereszty, **"Relationship between Anthropology and
Christology. St. Bernard, a Teacher for Our Age."** See pp. 46-76.
It shows the correlation between the stages in the mystery of Christ
and our spiritual development.

Study Questions

1. Explain the correlation between man's spiritual journey
and the stages of Christ's history in St. Bernard's thought.
2. Explain the notion of Wisdom in St. Bernard.
3. What is man's sin according to Anselm?
4. Why according to Anselm can God not forgive man without
requiring satisfaction?
5. Why does Anselm believe that the death of the God-man,
Jesus Christ, is the only appropriate satisfaction for our
sins?
6. Why according to Anselm can we not think of a greater and
more just mercy than the death of the God-man?
7. What is time-conditioned and what is of lasting value in
Anselm's theory?
8. How is the scholastic ideal of theologizing different from
that of the Fathers and of monastic theology?
9. Is Christology located where it should be in the *Summa* of
St. Thomas (in the Third Part, after grace and morality)?

10. Explain the basic principle of St. Thomas's Christology. Show how everything else depends on this one principle.
11. Why according to Thomas is the suffering of Christ greater than any human suffering?
12. Explain the five ways by which, according to Thomas, the passion of Christ has been instrumental in our salvation (by way of merit, satisfaction, sacrifice, redemption and efficient causality).
13. Explain how the whole sacred history of the Incarnate Word has caused our salvation according to Thomas.
14. Evaluate critically Thomas's Christology and Soteriology.

CHAPTER IV — CHRISTOLOGY OF THE REFORMATION

Recommended Readings

J. Dillenberger, C. Welch, *Protestant Christianity Interpreted through Its Development* (New York: Macmillan, 1988). It is a widely used history of Protestant thought.

P. Althaus, *The Theology of Martin Luther* (Philadelphia: Fortress, 1966). It remains a classic introduction to Luther's thought.

G. Aulén, *Christus Victor* (New York: Macmillan, 1931). It is still an influential Protestant interpretation of redemption.

Study Questions

1. How does Luther misunderstand the *communicatio idiomatum?*
2. Explain the existential starting point for Luther's theology.
3. How does Luther transform the *admirabile commercium* theme of the Fathers?
4. How does Luther transform the Anselmian notion of satisfaction?

5. What is the role of the humanity of Christ in our redemption according to Luther?
6. What are important new contributions to Soteriology in Luther's thought?
7. Explain the difference between the Lutheran and Calvinist view on the relationship between the divine and human natures of Christ.
8. What is the role of Christ the human being in our redemption according to Calvin?
9. How does the mediation of Christ precede his coming in the flesh according to Calvin?
10. Explain the prophetic and kingly office of Christ according to Calvin.
11. Explain the priestly activity of Christ according to Calvin.
12. Explain the work of our sanctification according to Calvin.
13. How is the Eucharist truly a communion with the flesh and blood of Christ according to Calvin?
14. Explain those principles of the Enlightenment which distort liberal Protestant Christology.
15. How does Kant reduce the major mysteries of Christology (in particular, the preexistent eternal Son, the incarnation and satisfaction) to presuppositions of the moral obligation?
16. How does Kant influence certain trends of contemporary christological thought?
17. How is Rahner's transcendental theological method influenced by Kant?
18. Explain Hegel's thought as opposed to, and yet dependent on, the Enlightenment.
19. How does Hegel explain the "immanent Trinity"?
20. Why are creation, incarnation, death and Resurrection necessary moments of a process according to Hegel?
21. Compare the principles of gnosticism with Hegel's philosophy.
22. What is the relationship between Christian religion and Hegel's philosophy according to Hegel?
23. What are the logical consequences of Hegel's system for theology?

24. What values can you see in Hegel's thought, that need to be transformed and integrated into Christian theology?
25. How does Schleiermacher defend Christianity against a rationalistic critique?
26. How, and on what basis, does Schleiermacher reinterpret all Christian teaching?
27. Did Schleiermacher make any lasting contributions to Christology? Explain.

CHAPTER V — PROTESTANT CHRISTOLOGIES IN THE TWENTIETH CENTURY

Recommended Readings

P. Ricoeur, "Preface to Bultmann," *Essays on Biblical Interpretation*, tr. P. McCormick (Philadelphia: Fortress, 1980), pp. 49-72. Although too uncritical of Bultmann, this thought-provoking essay explains well the three interrelated reasons for demythologization in Bultmann's hermeneutics.

H.U. von Balthasar, *The Theology of Karl Barth: Exposition and Interpretation*, tr. E.T. Oakes (San Francisco: Ignatius, 1992). Barth himself acknowledged this work to be an authentic interpretation of his theology.

C. Marsh, *Reclaiming Dietrich Bonhoeffer. The Promise of His Theology* (New York: Oxford Univ. Press, 1994). Marsh intends to prove that the immanent Trinity is in Bonhoeffer's theology the necessary background to the understanding of his Christology and ecclesiology. Examine the cogency of Marsh's analysis.

For information on contemporary Christologies see

J. Macquarrie, *Jesus Christ in Modern Thought*, pp. 293-335;

W.M. Thompson, *The Jesus Debate. A Survey and Synthesis* (New York: Paulist, 1985).

Study Questions

1. What caused the collapse of liberal Protestant theology in the first decades of the 20th century?
2. Who were the chief representatives of "crisis theology"? Characterize the common traits in these theologians.
3. How does Bultmann define myth? What is the function of myth for primitive man?
4. How does the mythology of the New Testament differ from other mythologies according to Bultmann?
5. What does Bultmann mean by the demythologization of the New Testament? Why is it necessary? (Explain the three reasons he gives.)
6. Why does Bultmann still cling to the historical event of Jesus Christ? What does he retain from Christianity?
7. Give a critical evaluation of Bultmann.
8. In what different directions did Bultmann's disciples move?
9. Contrast the radical crisis theology of the early Barth with his later Christocentrism.
10. How does Barth interpret soteriologically and existentially the traditional doctrine of the two natures of Christ and the hypostatic union?
11. How does Barth justify universal salvation?
12. According to Bonhoeffer how does the history of theology continue the passion story of Christ?
13. How does Bonhoeffer interpret the humanity and divinity of Christ?
14. How does Bonhoeffer interpret God's transcendence?
15. How does Bonhoeffer's Christology lead to his involvement in the anti-Nazi conspiracy and how does his imprisonment lead to a new development in his Christology (his "worldly" interpretation of Christianity)?
16. Evaluate critically Bonhoeffer's Christology.

PART III
SYSTEMATIC CHRISTOLOGY

INTRODUCTION

Recommended Readings

W. **Kasper,** *The God of Jesus Christ* (New York: Crossroad, 1984);

B. **de Margerie,** *The Christian Trinity in History* (Still River: St. Bede's Publications, 1982). These two books which provide an excellent historical and systematic treatise on the Trinity are most helpful for situating Christology in the right theological context.

K. **Rahner,** *Foundations of Christian Faith* (New York: Crossroad, 1978), pp. 138-175. The study of Rahner's view can stimulate a discussion on the universality of the offer of salvation and its concrete historical manifestation in Christ.

E. **Schillebeeckx,** *Jesus: An Experiment in Christology* (New York: Crossroad, 1981). On pp. 636-674 Schillebeeckx presents his systematic Christology. It would be worthwhile to discuss to what extent this last part is compatible with the author's reconstruction of the historical Jesus.

H. **Küng,** *On Being a Christian* (Garden City: Doubleday, 1976) pp. 119-478. Evaluate whether or not his christological method corresponds to that of Catholic theology. Why is his use of the critical historical method in conflict with the nature of Christian faith?

Study Questions

1. Discuss the criteria for a relatively successful christological synthesis.
2. Show by some examples how the existential questions of contemporary men and women need to be deepened and even transformed in order to receive an answer from the revelation of Christ.
3. Show how the mystery of the love of the Triune God provides coherence and intelligibility to the whole of Christology and Soteriology.

CHAPTER I — SIN AS A THREEFOLD ALIENATION

T.S. Eliot, "The Wasteland," "The Family Reunion," *The Complete Poems and Plays 1909-1950* (New York: Harcourt, 1958). These works are more powerful expressions of contemporary alienation caused by sin than any abstract theological treatise.

Study Questions

1. Explain sin as a threefold alienation. Try especially to show how in every sin we distort ourselves into a false absolute that causes conflict with other human beings. Show also that even an atheist or agnostic who commits a sin sins against God the Father.
2. What is the role of the body and the structures of society regarding sin?
3. How does the threefold alienation of sin, expressed in and through the body, carry with itself its own punishment?
4. Why, left to his own resources, can the sinner not extricate himself from his sin?
5. Why is it appropriate that we have been redeemed through God's incarnate Son?

CHAPTER II — THE MYSTERY OF THE INCARNATION

Recommended Readings

W. Kasper, *Jesus the Christ,* pp. 230-252. How does Kasper formulate the mystery of the hypostatic union? What notion of person does he use in expressing the mystery?

— **"Christology and Anthropology,"** *Theology and Church* (New York: Crossroad, 1989), pp. 73-93. How does Kasper see the relationship between Christology and anthropology?

E. Schillebeeckx, *Jesus,* pp. 636-674. How does Schillebeeckx formulate the hypostatic union? In what area(s) does his understanding deviate from that of the great christological Councils?

P. Schoonenberg, *The Christ. A Study of the God-Man Relationship in the Whole of Creation and in Jesus Christ* (New York: Herder & Herder, 1971); — **"Spirit Christology and Logos Christology,"** *Bijdragen* 38 (1977), 350-375.

Show the development of Schoonenberg's thought in these two studies. Why does he think it is necessary to reformulate the doctrine of the Incarnation? What are the ultimate consequences of his position?

K. Rahner, "Dogmatic Reflections on the Knowledge and Self-Consciousness of Christ," *Theol. Invest.*, vol. 5, pp. 193-215. Compare Rahner's theory with that of Lonergan.

R. Kereszty, "Psychological Subject and Consciousness of Christ," *Communio* 11 (1984), 258-277. It is a critical reappropriation of Lonergan's theory on Jesus' consciousness.

E. Johnson, *She Who Is. The Mystery of God in Feminist Theological Discourse* (New York: Crossroad, 1992). It provides a leading feminist theologian's perspective on God-language and the doctrine of God in Christianity. Compare it with my position on the feminist critique of Christology.

F. Martin, "Feminist Hermeneutics: An Overview (Part I & II)," *Communio* 18 (1991), 144-163, 398-424; **"Feminist Theology: A Proposal,"** *Communio* 20 (1993), 334-376. It is a reliable survey and critique of feminist theology as well as a proposal to move beyond its present *status quo*.

L. Bouyer, *The Seat of Wisdom* (Chicago: Regnery, 1965). Ahead of his times, Bouyer successfully reappropriated the insights of the Bible and Christian tradition on the role of woman in the economy of salvation. It remains an indispensable classic.

Study Questions

1. Explain the process by which God enters into a growing solidarity with his people as reflected in the writings of the Old Testament.
2. How does the very "logic" of solidarity call for the hypostatic union?

3. What explains the contemporary tendency to define the preexistence of the Logos in non-personal terms?
4. Why is the doctrine of the immanent Trinity a necessary condition for God's freedom regarding the Incarnation?
5. How does the Old Testament reject a direct transfer of sexuality into divine existence? What is the meaning of masculine and feminine traits or images applied to God?
6. How does the Church's Tradition express the transcendent character of divine fatherhood and sonship?
7. Provide some foundation for a theological anthropology of gender. (Starting point: Why do biological differences between man and woman have psychological and even metaphysical consequences?)
8. On what grounds does *JC* differentiate between (analogously) attributing masculine and feminine qualities to divine nature and (analogously) attributing masculine and feminine relationships to the Divine Persons as persons?
9. Regarding the ontological aspect of the hypostatic union, explain the following:
    a) How did the Revelation of God's Trinitarian life and the Incarnation revolutionize the understanding of "personhood" within Christianity?
    b) Define "person" in God.
    c) Explain the Incarnation of the Second Divine Person in ontological terms.
    d) Why does the *anhypostasia* of Jesus' human nature (his humanity not subsisting as a human "person" in the ontological sense) not result in a diminution of his humanity?
    e) Show that the mystery of the hypostatic union does not necessarily imply a contradiction
        (a) either on the part of the Son,
        (b) or on the part of human nature.
10. How can a modern understanding of person as consciousness and freedom lead to absurd consequences in Trinitarian theology and in Christology?
11. How should one understand person on the psychological level in order to perceive the correspondence between the

ontological and psychological aspects of the mystery of the Incarnation?
12. Define consciousness and its characteristics.
13. Define psychological subject and distinguish it from consciousness.
14. Distinguish between consciousness and self-knowledge.
15. Describe the relationship between psychological and metaphysical subject
    a) in general, and
    b) regarding Christ.
16. How should consciousness and psychological subject be predicated about the Trinity and Christ according to Lonergan?
17. How does the role of empathy in loving personal relationships help us understand the mystery of the Incarnation?
18. How can you show that the Incarnation fulfills human nature on an unexpected level?
19. Explain the Incarnation as a twofold existential process:
    a) the Word becoming a human being and
    b) the human being Jesus "becoming God."

CHAPTER III — THE HUMANITY OF THE SON

New Text
(Replace pp. 330-334 with what follows)

The divine knowledge of the Son is completely identical with that of the Father and the Holy Spirit. In Christology, however, we are not dealing with this eternal divine knowledge, nor with the Son's eternal divine consciousness, but rather with the nature and the different forms of his human knowledge as they are connected with his human consciousness. Thus, a review and expansion of what has already been outlined regarding the psychological aspect of the hypostatic union will become unavoidable.[13]

---

[13] See *JC* pp. 307-312.

As we have seen before, the purpose of the Son's Incarnation is complete solidarity with humankind. This purpose could not have been achieved had he not known himself, people, the world, and God in a human way.

a. The Common Human Knowledge of Jesus

No theologian today questions that Jesus had the same kind of experiential knowledge as all human beings.[14] Yet, just as his humanity serves to make the eternal Son humanly available for us, his common human knowledge also serves this purpose of mediation. Whatever Jesus learns about this world becomes for him a parable or symbol of God's world. Nonetheless, the transcendent reference of Jesus' experiential knowledge does not make it less human. His parables reveal him as a keen observer of nature and people, both of which he describes with vivid detail, humor, and sympathy. The budding seed of grain first produces the blade, the blade the ear, and the ear is filled with grain: Jesus depicts this process so graphically that, once heard, it engraves itself on the hearer's memory (Mk 4:28). He observes not only the processes of nature but also the life of people: the business venture of the merchant who risks all his wealth for one single precious pearl, the crafty dealings of the recently sacked manager, and the anxious waiting of the father who refuses to give up on his lost son are portrayed with the realism and imagination of an unusually sensitive observer.

As it happens to all human beings, the common human knowledge of Jesus was limited yet constantly growing. We have no reason to assume that Jesus knew more in the realm of natural sciences, history, or mathematics than any of his contemporaries who had been raised in the same cultural milieu. Even in questions of religious history which were of no consequence for his divine mission, Jesus shared the views of his fellow Jews. For instance, Jesus spoke of the Davidic authorship of Psalm 110 (Mk 12:36), not because out of modesty he concealed his superior

---

[14] While Jesus had the same kind of common human knowledge as we do, its concrete reality was transformed by its close link with Jesus' unique vision of the Father and the Father's inspiring and guiding activity.

knowledge of literary criticism, but because he sincerely but mistakenly believed that the Psalm was indeed the work of David.

b. Jesus' Knowledge of God

Both the synoptics and the Fourth Gospel affirm a unique knowledge or vision of God in Jesus.[15] According to Mt 11:25-27 and Lk 10:21-22, the mutual knowledge of Father and Son is of comparable breadth and depth, and consequently the Son's knowledge of his Father is unique and surpasses that of all creatures. Mk 13:32 also implies the Son's transcendent knowledge of the Father, while excluding the knowledge of the time of the parousia.[16]

We can also deduce Jesus' transcendent knowledge or vision of God from the hypostatic union: the human nature of Jesus is the Son's own human nature; consequently, it is appropriate for this human nature to share in a human way the divine knowledge of the eternal Son.

Jesus knew not only God himself with a unique intimacy but also revealed God's plan of salvation with an unparalleled authority. He taught not as the other rabbis, by interpreting the teaching of the rabbis before him, but in his own name, with a power and certainty that astounded his audience. His teaching is directly God's teaching (Mt 16:19; 18:18; Jn 8:26, 28-29).

At the same time, Jesus was growing in wisdom (Lk 2:52); his questions are not mere rhetorical devices, but show the limits of his knowledge. He even publicly acknowledges his ignorance about the exact date of the end of times (Mk 13:32).

Scholastic theology explained Jesus' knowledge of God as a special case of the beatific vision: in his earthly life Jesus was

---

[15] Cf. for instance, Mt 11:25-27; Lk 10:21-22; Mk 13:32; Jn 1:18, 5:20, 10:15, 14:7.

[16] "But of that day or hour, no one knows, neither the angels in heaven, nor the Son, but only the Father." The order 'angels,' 'Son,' 'Father' is an ascending one, going from the lower to the higher. This implies that the Son is above the highest creatures, the angels in heaven. Moreover, the statement about the Son's ignorance of the time of the parousia makes sense only if the disciples would otherwise have assumed that the Son knew this date. In other words, the Son's ignorance of this particular fact is presented by the gospel traditions as an exception to the supposed general sharing of knowledge between Father and Son. Cf. O. Cullmann, *The Christology of the New Testament*, pp. 286-288.

simultaneously *viator et comprehensor* (pilgrim on his way to God, and possessing the beatifying vision of God). He saw directly the essence of God on the higher plane of his soul and found supreme delight in it. Yet, this face-to-face vision and joy in the highest "part" of his soul did not prevent Jesus from suffering more than anyone else in the rest of his soul and in his body.[17] Regarding his knowledge of God's plan of salvation, St. Thomas taught that Jesus knew by direct divine inspiration or by infused knowledge (*scientia infusa*) what he had to reveal.[18] Scholastic Christology, however, does not treat the issue of Jesus' human consciousness.

It seems, however, more consistent with the scriptural data if, instead of explaining Jesus' unique knowledge of God in terms of the beatific vision, we derive it from his human self-awareness.[19] Through his human consciousness, it is the eternal Son who experiences himself in a human way, therefore his human consciousness must also include the awareness of his relationship to the Father since his Self as Son is constituted precisely by his being born from the Father. Thus, the self-awareness of the Son includes the awareness of his Father. This reasoning brings to light the unique character of Jesus' knowledge of God: he does not simply know or even see God the Son and God the Father as quasi objects distinct from himself (as the doctrine of the *visio beatifica* would require) but rather his immediate self-awareness includes his awareness of being the Son of the Father. At the same time, the above hypothesis accounts for the constant growth of Jesus' reflexive knowledge of himself and of the Father, since it does not presuppose a distinct objective vision of God's essence in which

---

[17] See St. Thomas, S.T. III, Q 46, a 8.

[18] Congar interprets S.T. III, Q 11, a 1 in this way. Cf. Y.M. Congar, *Jesus Christ* (New York: Herder & Herder, 1966), pp. 51-65.

[19] Here I have changed my opinion from the one I presented in *JC*. There, in addition to Jesus' self-awareness as the Son, I also assumed a direct (objective) vision of the Father in the earthly Jesus. But more reflection on Jesus' human self-awareness as always implying a direct awareness of his Father made me realize that the immediate objective vision would be a superfluous hypothesis which could not better explain any datum of revelation. (Lonergan maintains that Jesus had the beatific vision, in addition to his self-awareness, and my hypothesis of an immediate vision had been a modified remnant of Lonergan's position.)

Jesus would have had a comprehensive knowledge of God and of his plan of salvation from the beginning of his human existence. Human self-awareness is always immediate, global and luminous, but in need of clarification and gradual, conceptual articulation that will result in growing reflexive self-knowledge. In Jesus' case his growing reflexive self-knowledge, always including the knowledge of the Father, depends on the Father's constant guiding and inspiring activity. The Father and Jesus communicate in the Holy Spirit and Jesus reveals only what he hears from his Father in the Spirit.[20] We can better explain in this way why Jesus in his earthly life did not know the date of the end of human history: it was not part of the revelation the Son has received from his Father.[21]

The important role Jesus' common human knowledge plays in his mission appears clearly in this context. Neither his self-awareness as Son nor the Father's inspiring and guiding action through the Spirit dispense him from engaging his mind to the fullest as he contemplates in the Scriptures, in the events of his life, and in the reactions of people, the unfolding of his Father's plan and his own role in that plan. Through God's inspiration Jesus discovers and lives God's will from moment to moment, from one day to the next. The Father's inspiration ensures also that Jesus correctly understands himself, his Father and his own task in the Father's plan, and that he can express these divine realities in human words with infallible certainty. Thus the close cooperation of these three kinds of knowledge is necessary for the completion of Jesus' mission and explains in particular the power and depth of his parables. Through his direct intuition of God, every phenomenon of the world appears to him as pointing beyond itself: every created reality becomes an image or symbol of God's own life and of his plan of salvation. What he intuits of God's world he communicates to us through the images and stories he learned in a human way about our world. Through his inspired knowledge he is able to express infallibly through the words, images, symbols, and stories

---

[20] Cf. Lk 3:22, 10:21; Jn 3:22, 8:26, 8:40, 15:15.
[21] St. Bonaventure has already explained Jesus' vision of God along similar lines. See *In Sent.* III, D 14, a 2 qq 13.

of this world the invisible realities of God's life and plan of salvation.[22]

Recommended Readings

K. Rahner, "Christology Within an Evolutionary View of the World," *Theol. Invest.*, vol. 5, pp. 157-192. Rahner integrates the Teilhardian vision of the cosmic Christ into his Christology.

Study Questions

1. What is human nature and what happens when the Son assumes it as his own? How does the Incarnation change the concrete nature of every human being?
2. What does it mean that the Son has assumed a human nature (rather than the nature of an angel, animal or plant)?
3. What is the theological meaning of the *one* Incarnation? Why would it not be appropriate to have an Incarnation of the same divine Word in every culture or age?
4. How was Jesus fully human without original and personal sin?
5. Explain the human knowledge of Jesus (his common human knowledge, his knowledge of the Father and the

---

[22] Cf. Congar, *Jesus Christ*, pp. 63-65. At this point it might be useful to compare my hypothesis with that of Thomas. Instead of supposing a *visio beatifica* in the earthly Jesus, I assume that Jesus was aware of his divine identity and his own Father through his human consciousness. What Thomas called the *scientia infusa* of Jesus I see as a constant dialogue between Jesus and the Father in the Holy Spirit, a dialogue that guided and inspired every step of Jesus' life. In order to accomplish his saving mission, Jesus needed the close cooperation of his human self-awareness, the Father's inspiration in the Spirit, and his common human knowledge acquired from experience. I differ from Lonergan's position in that I do not see the need to affirm the beatific vision in Jesus in addition to his direct self-awareness as the Father's Son. In this regard my explanation is closer to that of Rahner. Cf. K. Rahner, "Dogmatic Reflections on the Knowledge and Self-Consciousness of Christ," *Theol. Invest.*, vol. 5 (Baltimore: Helicon, 1966), pp. 193-215.

Father's will, based on self-awareness and the inspiration by the Holy Spirit).
6. How do Jesus' growing common human knowledge, his direct intuition of the Father, and his inspired knowledge cooperate in carrying out his mission?
7. Why is it important for Soteriology that Jesus has a fully active human will?
8. Is the impeccability of Jesus' human will compatible with human freedom?

CHAPTER IV — REDEMPTION AS ASSUMPTION OF HUMANKIND INTO TRINITARIAN COMMUNION

Recommended Readings

J. Moltmann, *The Trinity and the Kingdom* (San Francisco: Harper, 1981). According to Moltmann, God becomes Trinity in Salvation History.

F. Varillon, *The Humility and Suffering of God* (New York: Alba House, 1983). How is Varillon's view different from the one adopted by Moltmann and by *JC*?

The three most important perspectives on the origin of sacrifice in the history of religions are presented in these three studies:

W. Schmidt, *Der Ursprung der Gottesidee*, vol. 5. *Endsynthese der Religionen der Urvölker Amerikas, Asiens, Australiens, Afrikas* (Münster, 1930-35);

M. Eliade, *The Sacred and Profane* (New York: Harcourt, Brace & World, 1959), pp. 99-104;

R. Schwager, *Must There Be Scapegoats? Violence and Redemption in the Bible* (San Francisco: Harper & Row, 1987). How could you reconcile the theories on the meaning of sacrifice in the works of Schmidt, Eliade, and Schwager with the phenomenological and theological approach of *JC*?

"Instruction on Certain Aspects of the 'Theology of Libera-

tion,'" by the Congregation for the Doctrine of the Faith, *Origins* 14 (1984), 193-204.

"Instruction on Christian Freedom and Liberation" by the Congregation for the Doctrine of the Faith, *Origins* 15 (1986), 713-728.

John Paul II, "Sollicitudo Rei Socialis," *Origins* 17 (1988), 641-660. These three documents together form the response of the Magisterium to the challenge of liberation theology. They point out the errors and dangers of some forms of liberation theology while stressing the need and outlining the principles for an integral theology of liberation.

J. Sobrino, *Christology at Crossroads* (New York: Orbis Books, 1979)

— *Jesus in Latin America* (New York: Orbis, 1987)

— *Jesus the Liberator: A Historical Theological Reading of Jesus of Nazareth* (New York: Orbis, 1993)

J.L. Segundo, *The Historical Jesus of the Synoptics* (New York: Orbis, 1985). Evaluate the above works from the eschatological perspective of Christian revelation. Do they respect the transcendent nature of God's Kingdom as God's gratuitous gift and as a share in the eternal life and joy of the Trinity?

J.P. Meier, "The Bible As a Source for Theology," *Proceedings of the Forty-Third Annual Convention of the Catholic Theological Society of America* 43 (1988), pp. 1-14. Evaluate the criticism of Meier on the use of Scripture in the liberation theologies of Sobrino and Segundo.

Y. Congar, *I Believe in the Holy Spirit*, vols. I-III (New York: Seabury, 1983). It is a monumental storehouse of biblical and historical theology on the Holy Spirit both in its Western and Eastern forms.

Study Questions

1. What is the logical connection between the hypostatic union and our redemption?
2. Regarding our redemption, under what aspect does God act as one, and under what aspect does each Divine Person have a different role?

3. What does it mean that the Father "gives" his Son? Compare it with a human father "giving" his son.

4. Explain the Father's compassion for humankind and for his Son. Why does compassion not contradict God's transcendent perfection?

5. How is the Father both the origin and the final end of our redemption?

6. How does Jesus enter into the threefold alienation of the sinner without assuming the guilt of any sin?

   a) How does he carry "the weight of our sins" more than we ourselves can?

   b) How does this entering into the threefold alienation of the sinner culminate on the cross?

7. Why is it impossible for Jesus to "suffer hell"?

8. Through the analogy of human death (we experience the death of our body as our own death), explore the meaning of our belief that God the Son himself died for us in our human nature.

9. How does the self-giving of Jesus to God on the cross reverse our alienation?

10. Describe the notion of sacrifice.

11. Why can only a human being offer a sacrifice to God?

12. Why is Jesus' sacrifice the only perfect sacrifice?

13. Give some of the reasons why redemption as satisfaction (atonement) is much questioned today.

14. Explain the meaning of "satisfaction" or "atonement" among persons. What ultimately satisfies for an offense against a person?

15. How is satisfaction (atonement) similar to sacrifice even among humans?

16. On what conditions does the gravity of an offense against a human person depend?

17. How can sin "offend" God? Is this notion of personal offense against God compatible with God's transcendence? Explain.

18. Show that, by demanding full satisfaction (atonement), God has treated us with respect as "adults" rather than acting out of vengeance.

19. Why are we, mere human beings, when left to our own resources, unable to offer a worthy satisfaction (atonement) to God for our sins?

20. Why is the most appropriate expression of this atoning love the death of Jesus?

21. How does the atoning sacrifice of Jesus restore the order of the universe?

22. Why does Jesus' satisfaction or atonement not work as a mere "balance of payments"?

23. How does the satisfaction or atonement of Jesus involve our cooperation?

24. Explain the role of the Holy Spirit
    a) within the Holy Trinity
    b) in the Incarnation
    c) in the earthly life and Passion of Jesus and
    d) in the Resurrection.

25. How is the sending of the Holy Spirit related to the Body (personal and ecclesial) of Christ?

26. Explain some of the basic principles of a Catholic liberation theology:
    a) The role of the Spirit in transforming hearts and society;
    b) Respect for the autonomy of economic and political realities.

27. Where did the Constantinian symbiosis of Church and society lead in the past and where might it lead in the future?

28. Explain the three complementary perspectives of biblical and patristic theology on the final goal of redemption.

29. How can one interpret the return of Christ in glory? What interpretation of "return" must be excluded?

30. Explain the eschatological state of the *totus Christus*. What is the relationship of the *totus Christus* to the Father? What (or rather who) guarantees the exclusion of a pantheistic interpretation?

31. How does our eschatological growing into the full maturity of Christ the man and into that of the perfect woman correspond to the dimensions of human nature?

32. Show that only the eschatological totality of all the saved achieves the perfection of every individual as a human being.
33. What is the theological reason for the conclusion that there will be a renewed material universe in the eschatological state?
34. What ensures that this new material universe has a continuity with the present one?
35. What could "redemption" mean for matter?
36. Explain the eschatological state of the material universe by two analogies (role of the human body and of the sacraments).

APPENDIX I — THE FINALITY OF CHRIST IN THE CONTEXT OF NON-CHRISTIAN RELIGIONS

Recommended Readings

J.A. DiNoia, *The Diversity of Religions. A Christian Perspective* (Washington: CUA, 1992). This book contains the most detailed bibliography on this issue (pp. 171-194). The theories on the relationship between Christ and non-Christian religions can be roughly divided into three categories: exclusive, inclusive and pluralist Christologies. The first is the position of fundamentalist Protestants: one can be saved only by an explicit faith in Christ. The second, in different varieties, has been well-represented in the Catholic tradition; in our age, Rahner formulated this position most articulately: if we accept our full humanity (ordained toward eternal life with God) we accept Christ who is our salvation. Lately, the pluralist approach became fashionable even in some Catholic circles: every world religion is an equally valid road toward God. Jesus is the unique and unsurpassable mediator of salvation for Christians. But this does not exclude an analogous role of Muhammad for Muslims and of Siddharta Gautama for Buddhists. The most vocal representative of this trend is Paul Knitter.

DiNoia tries a fourth approach: he affirms the irreducible diversity of religions. To what extent is his approach valid? Compare these four approaches to that of *JC*.

"Some Aspects of Christian Meditation" by the Congregation for the Doctrine of the Faith, *Origins* 19 (1989), 492-498. While not entirely negative, this instruction points out the dangers of an Eastern mysticism which, abandoning Christ, immerses itself into an absolute void and considers the mystical experience attainable by a variety of physical and spiritual techniques.

R. Gawronski, *Word and Silence. Hans Urs von Balthasar and the Spiritual Encounter between East and West* (Grand Rapids: Eerdmans Publishing, 1996). Compare Balthasar's approach to non-Christian religions with that of Rahner.

Study Questions

1. What can the history of religions conclude about Christianity's claim to be God's final and complete self-revelation?
2. What can one know about this issue only through the light of grace?
3. What unique features can historically be established about Jesus?
4. What is historically unique in the suffering of Christ?
5. How does the mystery of the Incarnation respond to man's longing for a simultaneously transcendent and immanent God? How is the Christian doctrine of the Incarnation different from the way other religions respond to the same problem?
6. What does the New Testament say about the uniqueness and finality of the Christ event?
7. What does the closing of the biblical canon in the second century say about the Church's belief in the finality of the Christ event?
8. What truth of divine revelation postulates that God's self-communication (which has reached its historical culmination in Christ) must have been available in some way to all human beings in all ages?

9. What is the double role of non-Christian religions regarding the mediation of God's revelation to all humankind?
10. What can a Christian learn about Christ from non-Christian religions?

APPENDIX II — CHRIST AND POSSIBLE OTHER UNIVERSES AND EXTRATERRESTRIAL INTELLIGENT BEINGS

New Text

Replace the first two paragraphs of this section (pp. 377-378) with the following text:

According to the revelation we have received, the final stage of cosmic and human evolution is Christ come to full stature who unites to himself humankind and through humankind the whole of material creation. Christ's goal, however, is the manifestation of the Father's glory in all creation and the transformation and mediation of the universe's praise and thanksgiving to the Father. Thus the transcendent entelechy (the universal moving force) of history is Christ and its final goal is God the Father. Nevertheless, according to the same revelation humankind is the center of God's loving concern and actions. The Father wants to adopt us as his children, the Son became a human being for our sake, died for our sake and has sent us the Holy Spirit.

In spite of all the above, we should not neglect (as most Christians have done in modern times) the important role of the angels in God's plan of salvation. Granted, the Bible presents the angels in the service of human salvation: they are God's agents and messengers for us. They watch with awe and longing the unfolding of the work of human salvation (1 P 1:12). "Surely (God) did not help angels but rather the descendants of Abraham" (Heb 2:16). Yet, the angels appear as higher beings than humans; they form the court and household of God and are "the sons of God."[23] They always see the face of God and praise God night and day (Mt

---

[23] God created all angels good. Even the fallen ones — Satan and his angels — serve, against their will, God's good purpose.

18:10; Rv *passim*). In the Gospel of Matthew the address, "Father in heaven," does not merely express God's transcendent fatherhood, but also points out the Father's heavenly court of angels. We pray that his will be obeyed on earth as it has already been among the angels of the heavenly court (6:10). The peacemakers will be called children of God in the sense that they will be counted among the angels (5:9). The just will be "like the angels in heaven" (22:30; cf. Mk 12:5; Lk 20:36). Thus, God's Kingdom did not originate here on earth: Jesus came to extend to the earth the Kingdom which has already been realized among the angels.[24]

Patristic theology and the Magisterium follow and unfold this view of Scripture. The Fathers also concentrate on the creation and redemption of humankind, yet their theology is far from being anthropocentric. For instance, the Nicene-Constantinopolitan creed further specifies "the heaven and earth" of the Apostles' creed: God is the creator of all visible and invisible creatures, our universe and that of the angels. According to several ancient theologians, men and women were created to replace the fallen angels. Thus, in their view humankind is not the crown of creation but a replacement for one missing chorus of the angelic world.

In the modern age, however, in order to preserve its importance, theology's central task became more and more the justification of human dignity. The doctrine on the angels first was organized by scholastic theologians into a separate treatise dominated by subtle metaphysical distinctions; then, in our lifetime it became the object of "benign neglect" on the part of the "cutting edge" theologians. It is most ironic that philosophy and theology turned anthropocentric exactly at the time when the natural sciences rejected the image of an anthropocentric universe and began to discover the unimaginably vast and complex dimensions of a fast expanding universe.[25]

---

[24] See D. Farkasfalvy, *Commentary on Matthew* in the making.

[25] In some sense, of course, theological anthropology should remain central for us: without discovering the fundamental orientation of human nature toward infinite goodness, truth and being, the revelation of the mystery of God will leave us indifferent. Moreover, without belief in the Trinitarian God of gratuitous love the foundations of human dignity are bound to collapse. Some scientists also postulate an "anthropic principle" at work in the evolution of the universe: the cosmic laws seem to be in favor of the development of intelligent

Recommended Readings

C.S. Lewis, *Out of the Silent Planet, Perelandra, That Hideous Strength* (New York: Macmillan, 1965). It is a religious science fiction trilogy that assumes the universal importance of the Son's Incarnation on our planet for other intelligent forms of life in the universe.

Study Questions

1. If there are other universes besides ours, what would their relationship be to the Father, the Son and the Holy Spirit?
2. What are the grounds (Scripture, Tradition, reasoning) for the book's conclusions regarding the response to the above question? To what extent are these conclusions conditionally certain (conditioned on the existence of "other universes")?
3. What is the range of theological possibilities for
   a) the existence or non-existence of intelligent extraterrestrial beings, and
   b) for their relationship to the Father, Son and Holy Spirit?
4. From a theological perspective, can there be intelligent extraterrestrial beings who are totally "alien" to us?

CONCLUSION

Study Question

How does the notion of communion (God entering through his Son into full communion with us, who are in the state of three-fold alienation, so that we may enter into full communion in the Spirit through the Son with the Father) provide the unifying center for such diverse images and notions as the Kingdom of God, the "marvelous exchange," the hypostatic union, and sacrifice?

---

life like ours (cf. P. Davies, *The Mind of God. The Scientific Basis for a Rational World* [New York: Simon & Schuster, 1992], pp. 200-222). However, the omission of the angels' role in Salvation History leads to the distortion of this history and makes it more difficult for theologians to create space for the role of possible extraterrestrial intelligent beings in God's universal plan.

RELATIONSHIP BETWEEN
ANTHROPOLOGY AND CHRISTOLOGY:
ST. BERNARD, A TEACHER FOR OUR AGE[26]

For our age Bernard's thought is particularly intriguing and relevant: on the one hand, he has thoroughly appropriated and synthesized the theological and spiritual heritage of the Fathers; on the other, he anticipates in himself our modern sensitivity. In full command of the Church's patristic heritage, he stands at the threshold of modernity. Thus he is uniquely qualified to help modern theology and spirituality in its twofold task of recovering the riches of tradition and "translating" it into the language of our age.

Bernard's central concern is personal and spiritual: how can the sinner return to God and be united with him? Although this intensely religious quest dominates his works, it does not restrict his vision of reality nor does it limit the genre of his writings to what we call today devotional literature. The student of his works can hardly avoid the conclusion that Bernard has thought through the ultimate theological foundations and philosophical implications of humankind's return to God. However, he has not written any single work which would systematize all of his doctrine. Moreover, while trying to capture the many aspects and individual nuances of our spiritual journey, up to the very end of his life he keeps changing his paradigms and the description of the different stages of our ascent to God. Nevertheless, behind the shifting images and concepts we can uncover an integral and consistent vision of all reality complete with a metaphysic, anthropology, epistemology and experiential psychology.[27] A fruit of continuous meditation on the Scriptures and the works of the Fathers, a result of interac-

---

[26] This essay is a revised form of the article published first in *Analecta Cisterciensia* 46 (1990), 271-299.

[27] I quote the works of Bernard according to the accepted abbreviations of the critical edition and use my own translation except for the epistles. The Roman number refers to the volume, the Arab number to the pages of the critical edition: *Sancti Bernardi Opera*, vol. I-VIII. Ed. J. Leclercq, C.H. Talbot & H.M. Rochais (Rome: Editiones Cistercienses, 1957-1977). Here follow the Latin titles of the works used in this article: Adv: *Sermones in Adventu Domini*; Ann: *Sermones*

tion with the Platonic heritage and with such contemporary theologians as William of St. Thierry and Hugh of St. Victor, this unified vision appears already in the *De Gradibus Humilitatis*, and, with some minor changes, remains constant throughout Bernard's career.[28]

Bernard's two overriding interests are God and his own personal self; but it is in Christ that he finds the key to understand both God and himself in the wider horizon of God's relationship to all humankind. Christology, then, in its twofold relationship to anthropology and theology, is the focal point of the Bernardine synthesis. On the one hand, the historical stages of Christ's redemptive work are structured according to the needs of fallen humanity; on the other, Christ gradually reveals and communicates God to the human race through the stages of redemption. We will, then, study Bernard's Christology in this twofold relation-

---

in Annuntiatione; Asc: *Sermones in Ascensione Domini*; Asspt: *Sermones in Assumptione*; Circ: *Sermones in Circumcisione Domini*; Conv: *Sermo de conversione ad clericos*; Csi: *De consideratione*; Ded: *Sermones in dedicatione Ecclesiae*; Dil: *De diligendo Deo*; Div: *Sermones de diversis*; Ep: *Epistola*; Epi: *Sermones in Epiphania Domini*; Gra: *De gratia et libero arbitrio*; Hum: *De gradibus humilitatis*; Mil: *Ad milites Templi*; Miss: *Homiliae super Missus est*; Nat: *Sermones in Nativitate Domini*; Nat V: *Sermo in Nativitate B. Mariae Virginis*; OS: *Sermones in festo Omnium Sanctorum*; Pasc: *Sermones in die sancta Paschae*; Pent: *Sermones in festo Pentecostes*; Pur: *Sermones in festo Purificationis B. Mariae Virginis*; SC: *Sermones super Cantica Canticorum*; Sent: *Sententiae*; IV HM: *Sermo in feria quarta Hebdomadae Sanctae*; XC: *Sermones in Ps. 90, "Qui habitat."*
Some valuable older English translations of Bernard's works include: *On the Love of God*, tr. T.L. Connolly (New York: Spiritual Books Associates, 1937); *Of Conversion*, tr. W. Williams (London: Burns Oates & Washbourne, 1938); *The Steps of Humility*, tr. G.B. Burch (Notre Dame: Univ. of Notre Dame, 1963). More recently, Cistercians Studies Publications (W.M.U. Station, Kalamazoo, Michigan) has undertaken the publication of the most important works of Bernard in English. See especially *CF* 1, 13, 19 *Treatises* I, II, III; *CF* 1A *Apologia*; *CF* 4, 7, 31, 40 *On the Song of Songs*; *CF* 13A *Steps of Humility and Pride*, *CF* 13B *On Loving God*; *CF* 19A *On Grace and Free Choice*; *CF* 19B *In Praise of the New Knighthood*; *CF* 25 *Sermons on Conversion*; *CF* 37 *Five Books on Consideration*; *CF* 53 *Sermons for the Summer Season*. The excellent translation of his letters is out of print: *The Letters of St. Bernard of Clairvaux*, tr. B.S. James (Chicago: Regnery, 1953).
28 Other aspects and paradigms of spiritual ascent are presented in *De conversione ad clericos, De Diligendo Deo, De Libero Arbitrio*, in the *Sermones Super Cantica*, and in his last major work, *De consideratione*. The results we obtain from studying these major works need to be complemented by the investigation of his sermons, whose genre ranges from highly elaborate literary masterpieces through mere outlines to actual sermons that have preserved the informal style of oral delivery to a living audience.

ship to humankind and to God in order to better understand its
significance for our contemporary theological and spiritual concerns.[29]

I. The Universality of Salvation and the Structure of Salvation History

With the Augustinian tradition St. Bernard stresses the consequences of our relationship to Adam: through generation we
all share in Adam's sin, which we also imitate by our personal sins,
and thus all experience concupiscence in our flesh and deserve
to die. Nevertheless, our relationship to Christ transcends in importance our relationship to Adam: our election in Christ has
taken place before the fall in God's eternity; our birth from God
overcomes the consequences of our fleshly descent from Adam
(Mil 23-25: III, 232-234).

---

[29] While the Christology and anthropology of Bernard have been extensively
studied, I know of no work which would have focused on their mutual corre-
spondence. Some of the major studies on Bernard's Christology: C. Bodard,
"*Christus-Spiritus*, Incarnation et Résurrection dans la théologie de saint
Bernard," *Sint Bernardus van Clairvaux, Gedenkboek*, Achel, 1953, 89-104; J.M.
Déchanet, "La christologie de saint Bernard," *Saint Bernard Théologien. Actes du
Congrès du Dijon, 15-19 Sept. 1953: Anal. S.O. Cist.* 9 (1953), 78-91; A. van den
Bosch, "Christologie bernardine," *Cîteaux* 9 (1958) 5-17; "Présupposés à la
christologie bernardine," *Ibid.*, 85-105; "Le mystère de l'Incarnation chez saint
Bernard," *Ibid.*, 10 (1959) 85-92; 165-177; 245-267. "Dieu rendu acessible dans le
Christ d'après saint Bernard," *Coll. Ord. Cist. Ref.* 21 (1959) 185-205; "Dieu
devenu connaissable dans le Christ d'après saint Bernard," *Ibid.*, 22 (1960) 11-
20; "Le Christ Dieu devenu imitable d'après saint Bernard," *Ibid.*, 341-355; "Le
Christ, Dieu devenu aimable d'après saint Bernard," *Ibid.*, 23 (1961) 42-57;
"Christ and the Christian Faith according to Saint Bernard," *Cîteaux* 12 (1961)
105-119; R. Kereszty, "Die Weisheit in der mystischen Erfahrung beim hl.
Bernhard von Clairvaux," *Cîteaux* (1963) 6-24; 105-134; 185-201. A. Altermatt,
"*Christus pro nobis.* Die Christologie Bernhards von Clairvaux in den *Sermones per
annum*," *Anal. Cist.* 33 (1977) 31-76. For Bernard's anthropology, see W. Hiss, *Die
Anthropologie Bernhards von Clairvaux*, Berlin, 1964. It would, however, be unfair
to omit the fact that in the above mentioned works the mutual relationship of
Christology and anthropology in Bernard's thought is affirmed and sometimes
emphasized. Thus, for instance, A. Altermatt states the relationship in this way:
"Das Zueinander des anthropologischen Rahmens (vgl. Voraussetzungen) und
der einzelnen christologischen und soteriologischen Inhalte bringt einen
durchgehenden Zug der bernhardinishen Theologie an den Tag" (*Die
Christologie Bernhards*, p. 155).

While no one may be sure of his or her own election and salvation, the Father's mercy embraces all humankind. He does not want the death of the sinner but his conversion and life. When the Father shows his mercy, he derives his cause and origin from his own nature; when he judges and condemns us, "in some way we force him to do so" (5 Nat 3: IV, 268. Cf. also Ep 77, 1.11: VII: 185.193). Christ, responding to the mercy of his Father, and mediating this mercy, has redeemed all human beings through his death.[30] His blood freed also those who died before his coming.[31] Thus, not only baptized Christians but the Jews and even the pagans had a chance to be saved through faith (Ep 190 18: VIII, 33). For the Jews this faith certainly meant a faith in the coming redeemer even though they may have had only a vague notion of him (Ep 77: 14: VII, 195). Lazarus in the Lukan parable symbolizes all the elect before the coming of Christ, and Lazarus is saved by his faith in the coming redeemer (Ep 190:18: VIII, 33). Moreover, *Letter* 77 defines faith in general as faith in God's promise to send a redeemer (Ep 77: 15: VII, 196). Therefore, Bernard probably holds that also the pagans are saved by some implicit faith in a redeemer:

> We believe that whoever were found believers among the nations, the adults were reconciled to God by faith and sacrifices while their children were helped only by the faith of the parents which, however, sufficed for them (Ep 77:4: VII, 187).

As shown above, in Bernard's vision **Salvation History is universal and Gods' mercy extends to all humankind in all stages of this history**. He cannot conceive of a God who would save only a few people before the coming of his Son. At the same time, however, Bernard maintains the privileged character of the time of the Savior's coming: this time alone is the time of grace. Those

---

[30] See, for instance, 28 SC 2: I, 193; 41 SC 6: II, 32; 1 Pur 2:IV, 335, 3 Sent 35: VIB 87, etc.

[31] But with the Fathers, St. Bernard holds that those just men who died before the death of Christ were held in the netherworld until Christ descended there to liberate them (cf. Adv 3:VIA, 11; 4 OS 1: V, 354-355).

who preceded the Savior received a blessing but its fullness was reserved for those who came after him (Ep 190, 18: VIII, 33). Bernard opposes the view according to which all the just of the Old Testament who were to be saved knew about "the time, manner and order of redemption" (Ep 77: 14: VII, 195). The knowledge of the mystery of salvation grew in the holy fathers as the time of the Savior's coming drew nearer. Yet even John the Baptist, greater than all the prophets, the friend of the bridegroom, still harbored doubts about the identity of the one who was to come (*Ibid.*, 13: 194).

The coming of Christ fulfilled the desire of all the just of the Old Testament. He was the kiss (the pressing together of the two lips, God and man into one) for whom all the just were longing (2 SC 3: I, 10).[32] When Christ began to teach, God opened his own mouth, the same God who used to open the mouths of the prophets in the Old Covenant (1 OS 7: V, 331). Through his blood, Christ redeemed all who were before him, and who came after him.

Bernard, then, concentrates on this privileged period of Salvation History, the mystery of the Incarnation, Death and Resurrection of the God-man, and shows how every phase of this one mystery serves the needs of the fallen human race. Thus, in order to understand the mystery of Christ we need first to get acquainted with these needs.

II. The Misery of Fallen Humankind: The Threefold Alienation

Human beings have been created *sui iuris*, that is, with the ability to possess themselves or determine themselves in freedom (Gra 36: III, 191). The ability of self-determination is the image of God in us, for God himself is absolute self-possession and self-determination. As the imprint in our soul of God's eternal being, this image is indestructible, and remains even in the state of sin, including eternal damnation (Gra 28; 31: III, 185-186; 187-188).

---

[32] Cf. the Vulgate text of the Song of Songs 1:1: "May he kiss me with the kiss of his mouth."

In the first sin, which has determined the human condition and which every individual sin personally appropriates, man and woman attempted to become gods on their own by determining through their own will what is right and wrong; thereby they usurped what belongs to the Word and Wisdom of God who alone determines by his peaceful will (*placida voluntate*) the order of the universe including the order of morality (Gra 33: III, 189; 3 Sent 94: VIB, 150).

The misery which has resulted from sin is not an arbitrary punishment inflicted upon the creature by a vengeful God, but is, rather, derived from the sinner's willful distortion of his own nature. We attempted to transcend ourselves by trying to acquire the wisdom of the Son through our own power. As a result, we fell below ourselves, we became flesh, that is, we are no longer capable of possessing ourselves in the truth, and even less capable of giving ourselves over to God and to our fellow human beings in love. The sinner's moral conscience (his *ratio* insofar as it represents the Word and Wisdom of God) condemns his false self-consciousness. Therefore, he does not want to face himself, runs away from self-knowledge and loses himself in sensing, knowing and craving the manifold material things of this world. If we had freely subjected ourselves to the order of God's Wisdom, we would have shared in God's Wisdom by God's gift. Since we wanted to become our own wisdom, we became a foolish beast. Instead of becoming like God, our senses and instincts dominate and enslave us, and our bodies drag us down. Thus the sinner who has opposed God finds himself necessarily in a multiple conflict with himself. He who does not want to be ruled by God, cannot rule his own body but is rather tyrannized by it. Moreover, the soul who loses God's life loses her ability to give life to her own body: Spiritual death will necessarily result in physical death. So the unity between the soul and body of the sinner has been broken, and has resulted in conflict and ultimate separation.

Not only did the harmony and unity of body and soul become shattered, but the very identity of the soul with herself was compromised by sin. The original simplicity, immortality and freedom of the soul could not be eliminated but it was covered up and distorted by opposite qualities. Her simplicity became obscured and contradicted by the many rationalizations through which reason tried to cover up the truth and escape from the inescapable judgment of her own conscience. Since she cut herself off from God's life, her immortality turned into a living death; her existence has become an unending process of dying, a *mors immortalis*. Her free will, the image of the Word in the soul, remains even in the state of sin insofar as her will clings voluntarily to what is evil. Yet she cannot will now what is truly good, because she has made herself her own prisoner: the will has freely imposed necessity on herself.[33]

In this state the sinner cannot know God because he ignores himself, the self-distorted but real image of God. Unable to face up to the truth of his situation, he rationalizes his sin by imagining a god who is either without holiness or without mercy (1 OS 13: V, 339; 38 SC 2: II, 15).[34] Thus, instead of knowing the true God whose very nature is love and mercy, the sinner fabricates an idol for himself.

The sinner is alienated not only from himself and God but also from his neighbor. Blind to his own sins, he acts as the Pharisee in condemning the tax-collector because he believes himself to be better than everybody else (Hum 17: III, 29). Whatever knowledge he has he abuses it to inflate his own ego. He cannot love anything but his own flesh, only what satisfies the needs of his body, flatters his vanity, increases his possessions and makes him appear greater in his own eyes (Dil 23: III, 138-139).

If we died in this state, the threefold alienation would become irreversible and eternal. Yet precisely this extreme danger of ours prompted the Son of God to become man and rescue us from this state of living death.

---

[33] Hum 28-30: III, 38-40; Gra 39-40: III, 194-195; Dil 36: III, 150; Mil 19: III, 230; 4 Asc 3-5: V, 140-142; 1 Adv 3-4: IV, 163-164; 3 Sent 94: VIB, 150; 81 SC 7-10: 288-291; 82 SC 1-7: II, 292-297.

[34] Cf. D. Farkasfalvy, "La conoscenza di Dio nel pensiero di San Bernardo," *Studi su San Bernardo di Chiaravalle nell'ottavo centenario della canonizzazione. Convegno internazionale Certosa di Firenze* (6-9 Nov. 1974) Rome, 1975: "Si può dire allora che anche per il peccatore il proprio stato di anima determina il concetto che si fa di Dio: nello stato di paura, di cattiva coscienza e d'orgoglio necessariamente si falsifica l'idea di Dio" (p. 208).

III. The Descent of God and the First Phase of Our Redemption

We can summarize the whole of Salvation History by paraphrasing the words of Bernard: In creation God gave ourselves to us, in the work of redemption he gave us himself, and, by giving himself, he restored us to our real selves; in other words, he reversed our threefold alienation (Dil 15: III, 132).[35] This total gift of God to us in Christ (and giving us in Christ the whole of creation) calls forth a reciprocal gift of our whole selves to God.

The Word's gift of himself takes place in history, and in various stages. Every stage of the Word's history effects in some way our salvation, and our spiritual development results in a gradual conformation to the incarnate, crucified and glorified Word. Bernard makes his own the Origenian principle: what happened once in Salvation History unfolds its effects everyday in individual souls. "The whole (mystery of the Son) is given to me, the whole is used up for my benefit" exclaims Bernard (3 Circ 4: IV, 284). Elsewhere he points out the saving function of every stage in Jesus' history by giving these words into his mouth:

> "I give you not only my conception but also my life; and I give you all this step by step through the stages of being a baby, a child, an adolescent and a young man; I add to it also my death, resurrection, ascension, and the sending of the Holy Spirit. This will happen so that my conception may cleanse your conception, my life may instruct your life, my death may destroy your death, my resurrection may precede your resurrection, my ascension may prepare your ascension, and the Spirit may strengthen your weakness" (2 Pent 5: V, 168).

There are two phases in the Word's history: The first is his descent, his self-emptying, which begins with the Incarnation and is consummated in Christ's death on the cross. The second phase is his ascent which begins with the Resurrection and is completed with the Ascension and Pentecost. Characteristically Bernardine

---

[35] "*In primo opere me mihi dedit, in secundo se; et ubi se dedit, me mihi reddidit.*"

in the description of the first phase is the close link between In-carnation and the cross: he can hardly speak about the mystery of the Son's birth without linking his birth to his death on the cross.[36] The birth marks the beginning of the Word's self-humiliation and self-emptying, the death its consummation. In the second phase the mystery of the Ascension dominates Bernard's attention be-cause Christ's Ascension to God causes **the** crucial transition in spiritual life, the transfer of the gravitational center of our affec-tions from the realm of the flesh to that of the spirit.

From Bernard's perspective the saving power of the Incar-nation is particularly important in what it does to the sinner's dis-torted relationship to himself, to his neighbor and to God. This threefold relationship constitutes a whole, both their distortion and healing takes place as a whole, but for the sake of clarity we need to analyze the three aspects both individually and in their interdependence.

As we have seen, man and woman have committed the first sin (from which every personal sin derives and which it imitates) in order to share in the knowledge of the Son. Created in the image of God the Son, they envied the Son's status and tried to become God by snatching away the type of knowledge and, in ul-timate analysis, the level of being which did not belong to them but to God alone. God did not fault the innate human drive for greatness, eternity and for sharing in God's life and glory (4 Asc 3: V, 139-140). However, he opposed the way by which man and woman attempted to assure this greatness for themselves, the boast-ing in their own power (4 Asc 6: V, 142-143). In the Incarnation the Son offered a saving alternative to our false way of striving for divine status. He presented himself to humankind in such a form that would bring salvation to all those who try to imitate him. By becoming a human being the Son became small and lowly, and thereby he showed how mistaken we were when we tried to imi-tate God by the way of pride (1 Adv 4: IV, 164). The Incarnation has revealed God's humility. The Word himself became the Word who cannot speak, the "*verbum infans*," poor, lowly and obedient to Mary and Joseph (1 Nat V 1: IV, 198; 3 Nat 2: IV, 259). Encoun-

---

[36] Cf. for instance, 1 Nat 8: IV, 251; 2 Nat 5: IV, 255; 3 Nat 4: IV, 261.

tering God as this little child, we who had aspired to greatness are called to convert and become like this little child, small, lowly and obedient.[37] Thus through the Incarnation the way toward a true self-understanding and true greatness is opened up for sinful man. Precisely because we aspire to be like God, we should imitate God in his humility.

God's humility goes beyond just becoming a small helpless child. It also includes God's free acceptance of the misery which we deserved for our sins. The Son has immersed himself into the universal misery of all humankind (IV Hebd S. 10: V, 63): he has taken upon himself not only a human shape but also the shape of a sinner; when circumcised, he was branded with the mark of an evildoer (3 Circ 3: IV, 283). He has taken upon himself not only the shape of a servant but that of an evil servant who deserves to be flogged. In fact the one who is completely innocent made himself into sin (SC 25: 9: I, 168; SC 71:11:II 22; IV Hebd S. 10: V, 61).[38] This "making himself into sin" means for Bernard that the Son of God has freely taken upon himself the necessary consequences of our sins which consisted in undergoing physical death and enduring the suffering that our sins inflicted upon him.

Even though the Son of God in his divine state had compassion for us without experiencing our wretchedness, he wanted to become wretched so that he might also experience it in himself. This experience was not necessary for himself but for us who needed to be convinced of his mercy (Hum 12: III 25). If, then, the Son of God has freely taken into himself our misery, how much more should we face up to our own misery and sinfulness, and accept them rather than try to escape from them by dissipating ourselves in finding pleasures through sense experience (Hum 13.28: III, 26.38)!

Moreover, as the Son of God made our misery his own out

---

[37] From the many texts which apply the *parvulus iste* of Mt 18:4 to Christ, see 1 Miss 5: IV, 17; 3 Miss 14: IV, 45; 4 NatV 9: IV, 226; 2 Quad 1: IV, 359; Pl 1: VIA, 28. See more on this topic in D. Farkasfalvy, "The First Step in Spiritual Life: Conversion," *Analecta Cisterciensia* 46 (1990), 65-84.

[38] Note that Bernard's version of 2 Cor 5:21 is different from that of the Vulgate: It is not God the Father who made Christ sin, but Christ "made himself sin" (*seipsum fecit peccatum*).

of love in order to learn compassion for us, we should also learn compassion for our neighbors. We suffer misery as a punishment for our sins. For us, then, the way to compassion for our neighbors is to feel their misery through our own and to find their mind in our own mind. In this way we identify with them to the point that we feel what is good or bad for them as if it were good or bad for us (Hum 6: III, 20-21). This compassion is the beginning of love for our neighbor and opposed to the attitude of the Pharisee who rejoices because he believes himself to be superior to the rest of humankind.

The Incarnation not only begins to restore the right relationship between ourselves and our neighbor, it also begins to restore our relationship to God. By learning to know ourselves in the truth we learn to know the Truth in ourselves, the Truth who is Christ. Since we have been created in the image of the Image of God, the Word, we cannot know ourselves in the truth unless we compare our wretched state to what we ought to have remained, the image of the Son. Then, by developing compassion for our fellow men and women who share in the same dignity of being created in the image of the Son and suffer the same misery and have the same need of forgiveness and healing as we do, we begin to discover the Truth who is Christ not only in ourselves but also in our neighbors; this is already the beginning of knowing God (Hum 14-18: III, 26-30). The final step will be to know the Truth not only in ourselves and in our neighbor but *in sui natura*, in Christ's own nature (Hum 6: III, 20-21).[39] This final step is only anticipated here on earth for short moments of ecstasy and reserved in its fullness for the eschatological state.

The above mentioned process moves from the sinner's flight from himself to self-knowledge in the truth and to the knowledge of, and acceptance of one's neighbor by means of contemplating, participating and imitating the humble Son of God made man. However, St. Bernard also develops another aspect of the restoration of our relationship to God: in *De diligendo Deo* and in various sermons the starting point is the fleshly love of the sinner who can love only himself and anyone else only because of himself, while

---

[39] Since for Bernard "Truth" is the very person of Christ, I translated "*in sui natura*" by "in his nature" rather than "in its nature."

the end point of the process is the spiritual love of those who love God for God's sake and themselves only for the sake of God. In the transformation of this love the Word made flesh plays a crucial role. God wants to save all human beings but he does not want to save them against their will. As long as we can experience only the threat of God and fear his punishment, we do not really know God in his own nature which is love and mercy; nor can we be saved by fear alone. Fear is the beginning of salvation, not salvation itself. Terror and force can move animals but cannot convert a human being:

> Intending to regain his noble creature God said: "If I force him against his will, I will not have a human being but an ass who did not come freely or gladly so that he might say: 'I will offer a voluntary sacrifice to you.' Should I give my kingdom to asses?" (Div 29: VI/1, 211)

So God tried another "experiment": he attempted to stir up humanity's desire for eternal life. But not even this appeal to our covetous nature moved our heart. Aware that love exerts the most powerful attraction for a human being, God then used a last approach. He began to attract, educate and transform our capacity to love:

> Seeing that all human beings became entirely entangled in the flesh, God revealed to them such a great sweetness in the flesh that they had to have a completely hardened heart if they did not love him with all their hearts. [...]
> So he came in the flesh and made himself so lovable that he gave us a love the greater of which no one has, namely, he gave his life for us. Whoever then refuses to convert will he not rightly hear: "What else should I have done to you and did not do it?" In fact nowhere else does God commend us his love so effectively as in the mystery of his Incarnation and Passion (Div 29, 2.3: VI/1, 211; 212).

God's power, strength and wisdom were all covered up in the Incarnation and Passion, but "his goodness could not have been

more abundantly revealed, more profusely expressed and more
clearly presented to us" (*Ibid.*, p. 212; cf. 1 Epi 2: IV, 293; 1 Nat 2:
IV, 245). Already for beginners the contemplation of the birth,
life and suffering of the Man-God (*Homo Deus*) is such an over-
whelming sweetness that it draws them to focus all their love on
him, and thus, in loving Jesus in the flesh, they already love God
himself in the flesh. If beginners persevere in this contemplation,
they will gradually see and savor in Christ's human love the divine
love of God the Father himself. Already the infant Jesus shows us
the heart of the Father: "Such is the heart of God the Father for
us as it has been disclosed by the one who came from the Father's
heart" (2 Epi 4: IV, 304; cf. also 2 Pent 3: V, 167). Nevertheless, it
is on the cross that through the wounds of Christ the ultimate
depth of God's love is shown to those who are able to perceive it.
Bernard's approach to the heart of Jesus differs somewhat from
the modern devotion to the Sacred Heart. For him the pierced
heart reveals ultimately not the human love of Jesus, but the "bow-
els of God's mercy":

> The secret of his heart lies open through the holes of
> his body; that great mystery of love lies open, there lie
> open the bowels of God's mercy in which the Rising Sun
> from on high has visited us (61 SC 4: II, 150-151).

In other texts Bernard explains also the Trinitarian dimen-
sion of God's love: "*Cor Sponsi cor Patris sui*" (SC 62: II, 158, 158):[40]
the heart of the Church's bridegroom opens up for us the heart
of his Father.

Once we begin to appreciate the love of the crucified Christ,
we want to be crucified with him, which, according to Bernard,
would draw us to a Cistercian monastery.[41] The sweetness that
comes from contemplating the passion of the Son of God in the
flesh makes it possible for the monk to remain on the cross and
be conformed to the suffering of Christ until the very end of his
life.[42]

---

[40] Cf. also "*Profecto enim tale est cor Dei Patris erga nos, quale nobis expressit qui de corde eius processit*" (2 Epi 4: IV, 304).

[41] 21 SC 2: I, 123; 3 Sent 1: VIB, 59-60; 3 Sent 119: VIB 216

[42] 1 And 3: V, 428-429; 1 Pasc 8: V, 83-84.

IV. The Mystery of Redemption: Liberation, Satisfaction, Sacrifice, Buying Us Back at a Precious Price

However, if the passion and death of Christ were nothing but the mere revelation of God's love for us, we could not be conformed to his suffering, and consequently, we could not be saved. Although Bernard treats with preference the passion and death of Christ as the ultimate expression of God's love for us, he is fully aware that our redemption consisted in more than a mere revelation of God's love. Christ's love for us results from his love for the Father for whom he has intended to save humankind (1 Adv 4: IV, 164) and whom he has reconciled to us by the outpouring of his blood. His blood has become a most pleasing sacrifice to the Father; it has satisfied for our sins and thereby obtained for us forgiveness from the Father and liberated us from the power of the devil. This redemptive work of the Son made man, described interchangeably as liberation, satisfaction, sacrifice, or "buying back" (the original meaning of *redemptio*), insofar as it constitutes an impenetrable mystery is called by Bernard *sacramentum redemptionis*. Bernard always presupposes its truth but does not speak about it at length in his major works. However, when he feels that this *sacramentum* is belittled or denied, he comes out in full strength to defend it. We see Bernard's passionate defense of the traditional doctrine of redemption in the letter he addressed to Innocent II against the errors of Abelard (Ep 190).[43]

---

[43] See especially Ep 190, 24-25: VIII, 37. It is a well-known fact that not only Abelard but also Anselm rejected the patristic notion of redemption from the devil's rightful dominion through the death of Christ. According to the patristic theory we have been justly held under the devil's power since we had freely subjected ourselves to his dominion. Thus it was appropriate for God to free us from the devil's power in a just way, i.e., by the death of the innocent Jesus whom the devil unjustly tried to subjugate by putting him to death. Anselm replaces this interpretation with his theory of satisfaction. Bernard, however, retains the essentials of both the traditional theory and that of Anselm, but rethinks both of them, as it most clearly appears in his controversy with Abelard. He explains the underlying truth in the patristic speculation about the alleged "rights of the devil over sinful humankind": the devil's dominion over the sinner is just but not his will by which he wickedly acquired dominion over him. Ultimately, the justice belongs to God who allowed sin to result in its necessary consequence, the sinner's subjection under the devil (Ep 190, 14: VIII, 29).

Abelard's critique of redemption which Bernard quotes in
his letter to Innocent II sounds surprisingly contemporary:

> To whom does it not appear cruel and wicked that any-
> one should require the blood of an innocent person
> as some kind of a price, or that anyone in any way
> should be pleased by the murder of an innocent per-
> son? How, then, could God find the death of his Son
> so acceptable as to be reconciled by it with the whole
> world? (Ep 190, 22: VIII, 36)[44]

In his reply Bernard explains that God did not thirst for the
blood of his Son but for our salvation which was in the blood; nor
did he require the blood of his Son but accepted it when it was
offered to him. In Bernard's theology, Christ's will to satisfy for
our sins comes from the Son's initiative rather than as an act of
obedience by the Son to the Father. The sin of humankind has
led, necessarily, according to the order of reality, to both physical
and spiritual death. The Son, out of love for his Father and for us
sinners, decided to become man and die in the sinner's place and
for the sinner's sake. Being innocent, he died freely and
undeservedly. Being the Son of God made man, he has united
himself to all of humankind as head to his members, and so he
could satisfy for all of us and could free us all from both physical
and spiritual death.[45] Thus, in the Son's mission the requirements
of both justice and mercy were fulfilled (1 Ann 9-14: IV, 22-29; 3
Sent 23: VIB, 81-82).

St. Bernard also speaks at times about the redemptive work
of Christ as sacrifice, but he does not restrict Christ's sacrifice to
the crucifixion. He most often combines the birth of Jesus with
his suffering on the cross. According to III Pur 2-3, Jesus offered
himself to the Father as the most precious morning sacrifice when,
as an infant, he was presented in the Temple. His self-offering on

---

[44] Bernard quotes Abelard's *Commentary on the Romans* II, ed. Buytaert, vol. I, pp.
117-118.

[45] Not that we do not have to undergo physical death but our physical dying will
become for us the way to everlasting life (Ep 190, 15: VIII, 29-30; 1 Adv 4-5: IV,
163-165; Mil 23-28: III, 232-236).

the cross, the evening sacrifice, has only completed the first offering in the Temple.

The above themes of redemption as liberation, satisfaction, and sacrifice receive inner coherence and intelligibility if we understand them with St. Bernard as the victory of divine love over evil. Just as the dying flies cannot eliminate the sweet ointment, the blasphemies and insults of those who killed the Son of God could not stop the flow of the sweet ointment from the side wound of Christ. On the contrary, the Jews were stones who hit a softer stone from which the sounds of love echoed forth and the ointment of love poured out in abundance (IV HM 8-9: V, 62-63). In other words, the murder of the Son of God which made the whole world turn pale and tremble and almost made everything turn back to the state of primordial chaos, this worst sin of all, became the means of redemption:

> He who made himself into sin endured this death in himself, so that he might condemn sin by sin. For in this way all sins, both original and personal, were deleted and this particular sin was eliminated by itself (*Ibid.*, 7: V, 61).

This could happen because the insults Christ endured called forth in him not only a patient but a generous, overabundant love in which he asked his Father to forgive his executioners. His divine word did bring about for what it had been sent, the Father's forgiveness. Thus Christ was not merely not conquered by evil, but he in fact conquered the evil with good (*Ibid.*, 8-9: V, 61-63). Salvation is then in the blood of Christ not by way of some magic force but because the outpouring of his blood is the expression of a love the greater of which no one can have. It obtains forgiveness from the Father and transforms the hearts of his executioners.

It is here that Abelard and Bernard part company. A superficial reading of their respective texts makes the reader wonder why, in spite of the same emphasis, Bernard is so vehemently opposed to Abelard. After all, both emphasize the life, suffering and death of Jesus as the manifestation of divine love for us and as an example to imitate. However, Abelard is ambiguous on the saving effect of Christ's cross: he does not clearly affirm that Christ's death saved us from the power of the devil and, to my knowledge, never mentions the satisfactory value of Christ's death for us. In his own individualistic frame of mind Abelard cannot understand how the death of the innocent Son of God may obtain forgiveness for us sinners from the Father. For Bernard, however, who sees Christ in a mysterious unity with all humankind (as the head of his Body, the human race), such satisfaction for others is intelligible and belongs to the very heart of the Christian faith. If Christ's death had not satisfied for our sins, if it had not obtained forgiveness from the Father and liberated us from the power of the devil, we could not participate in the love of God, and, consequently, we could not imitate Christ.[46] From this perspective those texts of Bernard which speak about God's efforts to call forth a response of love in us receive a new depth: they should not be interpreted simply according to the paradigm of a human call for love, a call that remains outside the person who is called. Since Christ died for us, God works in the heart of the sinners an inner transformation, a new birth; he recreates us by sending his Spirit into our hearts so that we may return God's love in and through his Spirit (cf. Ep 107:6: VII, 273 & XC 9, 3: IV, 437).[47]

Bernard does indeed agree with Abelard that Jesus came to show us an example of humility and love. But without the sacrament of redemption (the work of satisfaction to the Father, liberation from the power of the devil and the inner transformation of the sinner by the Holy Spirit) the former would be of no value for us. If we are not forgiven and liberated from the power of the devil and death, if we do not receive a share in the humility and love of Christ, how can we imitate them?

---

[46] For Bernard the redemption of Christ works a true ontological transformation in us prior to any response of love. Therefore an infant is saved by the "sacrament of redemption" even though he is still unable to express his love. Infant baptism thus becomes the "litmus test" which brings to the fore the real disagreement between Bernard and Abelard (cf. Ep 190, 24: VIII, 37).

[47] We must admit that — contrary to Bernard's accusation — Abelard does speak about our love for God as the work of the Holy Spirit in us. However, I have not found any Abelardian text which would explain that the outpouring of the Holy Spirit into our hearts is the result of the saving death of Christ.

So he taught justice but did not communicate it to us;
he showed us love but did not pour it into us; and then
he just returned to his own? (Ep 190:17: VIII, 31)

Thus, according to St. Bernard the humility, the virtues and
especially the love of Christ can only be imitated if they are first
participated in; and they can be participated in only as a result of
Christ's death on the cross which obtained the forgiveness of our
sins. The following passage summarizes clearly both the affinity
and the difference between Bernard's position and that of Abelard:

I perceive three important aspects in the work of our
salvation: the form of humility by which God emptied
himself; the measure of love which he extended up to
death, even to death on the cross; and the sacrament
of redemption in which he took away death by enduring it. The first two without the last may be compared
to trying to paint upon nothing. Great and necessary
is indeed the example of humility, great and most worthy to accept the example of his love. However, if there
is no redemption, the first two remain without foundation and therefore, they cannot stand. I want to follow
the humble Jesus with all my efforts; I want to embrace
the one who loved me and gave himself over to me with
the arms of a reciprocating love. But I need to eat the
Passover lamb. For unless I eat his flesh and drink his
blood, I will not have life in myself (*Ibid.*, 25:38).

Eating his flesh and drinking his blood means for Bernard
not only Eucharistic communion but our manifold participation
in the true Passover Lamb on whose sacrifice our participation in
the life and love of Christ depends.[48]

---

[48] The limits of this article prevent me from a detailed discussion of Abelard's views
on redemption. I believe that Bernard rightly perceived and rejected a rationalistic tendency in Abelard's soteriology (the reduction of the mystery of
redemption to a mere example of divine love for us) without noticing or
acknowledging that Abelard himself did not follow up consistently on his own
reductionism and that in some texts he maintained the traditional views. See on
this A.V. Murray, *Abelard and St. Bernard. A Study in Twelfth Century 'Modernism'*

V. The Ascension of Christ and Our Ascension

The death of Jesus is, then, the focal point of the mystery of our redemption. Our gradual conformation to Christ, which begins by becoming like the child Jesus and continues through our Ascension with Jesus, is seen by Bernard as a real participation in his mysteries, and this participation was made possible by Christ's redemptive death.

As we have seen above, through the Incarnation, earthly life, and especially through the passion of Christ, we reach God himself; everything in the history of the Word incarnate, the infant Jesus, the preaching, the miracles but especially the pierced side of Christ reveal and communicate God to us. Yet until we have experienced the Ascension of Christ, God's humility, goodness and love as mediated to us through the life of the earthly Jesus will call forth in us only an emotional love (*amor cordis*) which, in some way, is only an *amor carnalis*, a "fleshly love." This should normally develop into an *amor rationalis*, a love ordered according to the right judgment of reason.[49] Even though the *amor carnalis et rationalis* reaches God himself through the man Jesus, it is still fleshly, because it is moved only by the memories of the Word's history in the flesh. It is through the *dulcedo*, the attraction of the

(Manchester: Manchester Univ. Press, 1967), 117-130. In the same book, however, Murray misrepresents Bernard's position by reducing it to a misleading statement: "In short, Bernard looks on the work of Christ as a transaction (between God, Christ and the devil) and Abelard does not" (p. 117). Murray does not perceive the most important insight in Bernard's understanding of redemption: The death of the Son effects our redemption not as a juridical transaction, not even because of the infinite dignity of the person of the Redeemer (as in Anselm's theory) but because the Son's dying expressed his almighty love for the Father. For a somewhat different evaluation of the positions of Bernard and Abelard on redemption see F. Gastaldelli's comments in *Lettere 1-210, Opere di San Bernardo* vol. VI/1 translated by E. Paratore, commentary by F. Gastaldelli, Milan, 1986, pp. 808-812, with further bibliography on p. 812. (Gastaldelli, however, seriously misrepresents western Soteriology by stating that "Fino al secolo XI, la teologia occidentale era attestata pressoché esclusivamente sulla soluzione proposta da Origene, che considerava l'uomo decaduto come un proprietà del diavolo e la redenzione un riscatto..." p. 808-809. What about redemption as "*admirabile commercium*," as sacrifice, what about the saving efficacy of all the mysteries of the earthly life of Christ? All these soteriological themes have been the common patrimony of western patristic thought and remained alive up to the high middle ages.)

[49] Div 29,1: VIA, 210-211; 20 SC 49: I, 116-121.

flesh of the incarnate Word that the soul has her first taste of God's attractiveness. This love is so emotional that it is prone to exaggerations; it is somewhat blind and can easily fall prey to heresies or at least to an extreme asceticism, and, therefore, it needs the tempering, ordering, sobering activity of a reason enlightened by faith.[50]

However, the risen Christ as he is in himself cannot be reached by the *amor carnalis et rationalis,* just as he can no longer be perceived by our senses in the state in which he actually is. He is no longer in the form of the slave which could have been the object of sense experience. He exists now in the glory of the Resurrection and is sitting with his Father on the throne of glory. In the state of glory Jesus has not divested himself of his humanity nor even of his flesh; but this flesh is of a different kind, a heavenly flesh which is no longer susceptible to suffering and death (28 SC 10: I, 198). It is no longer a lantern that screens the blinding light of the divinity, but has become completely transparent so that it reveals the divine beauty, the infinite dimensions, the length, the width, the height, and the depth of the Son's divinity.[51] Thus, when he appears to Mary Magdalene, he cannot show himself as he is now in his divine glory but rather adjusts himself to her sense experience, by presenting himself in the form of the slave so as to comfort her weak faith.[52]

In Bernard's theology the Resurrection of Christ receives much less emphasis than his Ascension.[53] The latter is crucial for Bernard because he attributes to it a decisive influence on the spiritual ascent of the soul to God. Bernard knows that God's way of transforming us by his grace corresponds to the sinner's psychological condition. For Elisha to receive the spirit of Elijah it was essential that he actually see Elijah taken up to heaven. The

---

[50] 20 SC 9: I, 120-121; 50 SC 4: II, 80; Div 29:1-4: VIA 210-213.

[51] 3Asc 3: V, 132; 6Asc 11: V, 156; 3 Sent 93: VIB 150.

[52] Bernard gives these words into the mouth of the risen Christ: "*Adhuc quidem tuis sensibus gero morem, formam ingerendo servilem, quam de consuetudine recognoscas*" (SC 28:9: I, 198).

[53] In the critical edition there are four sermons *De Resurrectione,* six *De Ascensione.* However, the third and fourth sermons *De Resurrectione* do not treat the theme of the resurrection. See on this theme, J. Leclercq, "Le Mystère de l'Ascension dans les sermons de Saint Bernard," *Collectanea Cisterciensia* 15 (1953), 81-88.

psychological experience of this vision made him ready to enter a new stage in spiritual life so that he could receive a double portion of Elijah's spirit. Thus, for the disciples it was essential to see the Lord ascending in the flesh so that all their affection which had long been centered on the Lord's flesh might be taken up with him into heaven and be purified of the limitations of fleshly love. They had to be deprived even of the presence of the pure flesh of Jesus in order to be ready to receive the fullness of the Spirit who changed their *amor carnalis et rationalis* into *amor spiritualis*.[54] From that point on they were able to "taste" not only the sweetness of God's love as manifested in the flesh, but also Wisdom's sweetness which is the "taste" of truth, justice and goodness (20 SC 8, I, 120). All believers have to go the same route. Only if we "see" Christ ascend into heaven can our love be purified and changed into spiritual love.

The Ascension changes not only our love but also our faith. An incipient faith which clings to the memory of Christ's presence in the flesh, a faith weighed down by sense experience, is to be transformed into a faith which transcends the limits of the senses, embraces the infinite dimensions of Christ's divinity, and touches with its fingers the one who is transformed into divine beauty and endowed with God's majesty and glory (28 SC 9: 910: I, 198-199).

Nevertheless, the perfect soul who has ascended with Christ to the realm of the spirit, does not abandon the *memoria* of the mysteries of the Word made flesh. On the contrary, she discovers ever more the divine love opened up for us in the wounds of the crucified Jesus. Her prayer life is stretched out between the two poles of *memoria* and *praesentia*: she recalls the mysteries of the earthly life of Jesus in order to enkindle her desire for the presence of the glorified Lord (Dil 7-12: III, 124-129).[55]

---

[54] We say fullness of the Spirit because no one can love the flesh of Christ, more precisely, no one can love the Man-God in the flesh without some participation in the Spirit of Christ (20 SC 7: 1, 119).

[55] Cf. "... il Cristo terreno del passato, conservato nella memoria è soltanto un gradino verso il Cristo glorioso attuale, vivo ed accessibile in maniera spirituale... Allora il punto di partenza è il Cristo terreno in cui la natura umana è nello stesso stato mortale e misero come in noi stessi, ma il punto di arrivo e il Cristo glorificato in cui l'umanità non è più un'ombra o un ostacolo perchè già inclusa nella gloria divina." (D. Farkasfalvy, "La conoscenza di Dio," pp. 212-213.)

The soul who, in an incipient way, begins to know the Christ of glory already here on earth, no longer fears to be rebuked and crushed by divine glory since she no longer tries to grab God's wisdom and glory by her own power; she has learned to share in the humility and love of the incarnate and crucified Son who himself did not cling to his divine glory and divine state of being but emptied himself for our sake (62 SC 4: II, 157-158).

The "deification" of the man Jesus does not mean a loss of his human nature or even flesh, but rather a deification of his affections (Asspt 1: V, 262). Both his body and his affections have been glorified. This means that he can suffer neither in the body nor in his soul. Yet he does not neglect those who are still struggling and suffering on earth. He loves those who suffer without himself suffering or being disturbed. This mystery of divine affection is far above our experience; it means mercy without experiencing misery, compassion without passion (SC 26:5: I, 173). The glorified Christ can only rejoice, yet his love for us who still suffer on earth is unspeakably greater and more effective than the compassion of the apostle Paul on earth who rejoiced with those who rejoiced and wept with those who wept (Div 34:5: VI/1, 232).

A superficial reading of St. Bernard's works may suggest that the flesh of Christ has a function only for the beginners in spiritual life; for those who are truly "spiritual" the flesh of Christ is of no use; they contemplate only Christ the Truth, Justice and Wisdom. In reality, however, St. Bernard sees an important role for the glorified flesh of Christ. The angels in heaven had thirsted for the presence of Christ in the flesh and their desire has been fulfilled in the Ascension. Bernard, to my knowledge, never provides a direct explanation for this desire of the angels; yet we can surmise the reason for it from what Bernard likes to present as the goal of God's love, to unite perfectly and definitively the highest with the lowest: *summa imaque consocians* (Csi 2,18: III, 426; cf. also 2 Nat 4: IV, 254). With the Ascension of Christ and Pentecost, then, a most faithful and most gratifying exchange and union between heaven and earth has been consummated: "The Spirit is on earth, the flesh is in the heavens and from now on all share all things in common for ever" (3 Pent 2: V, 172).

By contemplating the Ascension of Christ and receiving the

fullness of the Holy Spirit at Pentecost, we anticipate already here
on earth our Ascension into heaven. To the extent that we love
the glorified Christ for his own sake (rather than for a reward other
than love itself), we become the "spouse" of the Word, or rather
we realize in ourselves the love of the one unique Spouse, the
Church.[56] To the extent that we pass into God and become one
spirit with God, we come into our own perfection and beauty, and
the Word/Bridegroom will find in us his desired and unique
Spouse. What the Word desires in his spouse is not her good will,
knowledge, virtue or wisdom, but her beauty; this beauty comes
from the soul's regaining her similarity with the Word. Just as the
Word is the shining splendor and form of God's substance (*splendor et figura substantiae Dei*) insofar as he is Truth and Wisdom, so
the beauty of the soul consists in her conscious conformity to the
Word as Truth and Wisdom. "The Truth shines in her mind and
the mind sees herself in the Truth."[57] This beauty may also be
called the *honestum*: the serene self-possession of a purified conscience who is not aware of any guilt and attributes all her wisdom
and beauty to God.[58] The beauty of the Spouse which the Word
desires is this shining light (and there is nothing brighter than this
light) of the soul's self-awareness. She sees herself as modest, shy,
and fearful while firm in her resolve not to commit anything that
might spoil the glory of her conscience (85 SC 10: II, 314). Here
we have arrived at the counterpoint of the first stage in spiritual
life: at the beginning of conversion the sinful soul must face the
truth in herself and face herself in the truth, the result of which is
intense suffering, shame and confusion. At the end of the spiritual ascent, however, the threefold alienation has ceased: when
facing the truth in herself, the soul is filled with the humble self-

---

[56] 74 SC 10: II, 239; 83 SC 5: II, 301; 2 O Epi 2: IV, 320. ✱

[57] "*veritas in mente fulget, et mens in veritate se videt.*" (SC 85:10: II, 314). See also 3 Asc
3-5: V, 132-134; 6 Asc 12: V, 157; 6 Asc 14-15: V, 159.

[58] One should write a monograph on the beauty in St. Bernard's theology. The
decor of the soul has many meanings related to the one that is explained in
detail in 85 SC10-11. It is also called by Bernard a combination of innocence and
humility, or purity and humility, the purity of intention which intends the truth
for the sake of loving the truth (45 SC 23: II, 50-51; 62 SC 13: II, 160; 74 SC 10:
II, 245). Cf. also Ep 113:4-5: VII, 289-290 in which Bernard lays down a philosophical foundation for the theology and morality of beauty in human beings).

awareness of her beauty and dignity; she is at peace with herself, with her neighbor and with God.

We see here the twofold paradox of what we may call the eschatological humanism of Bernard. The Spouse becomes fully beautiful in herself when she has been fully conformed to the Word. She flourishes when she does not keep anything to herself but shares all of herself with her Bridegroom (7 SC 2: I, 31-32). She remains beautiful as long as she acknowledges that all her beauty comes from God. The peace and joy of her human consciousness is the result of God's Wisdom that fills and transforms her. Moreover, the individual soul comes into her own full perfection and beauty to the extent that she realizes in herself the features of the one Spouse, the unique dove, who is the Church of Christ. Thus the individual soul must lose herself in a twofold way, both in Christ and in the Church in order to develop her very own beauty.

Here on earth, however, this state of becoming the fully purified spouse is never completely and permanently attained. Up to the end of his life St. Bernard remains acutely aware of himself as a sinner. In his last letter he begs his friend to pray for him:

> Pray our Savior, who wills not the death of a sinner, that he will not put off my timely departure, but that he may watch over me in my passing. Support, I beg you, with your prayers a poor wretch destitute of all virtue, so that the enemy who lies in wait for me may find no place where he can grip me with his teeth and wound me (Ep 469).[59]

To the extent that the soul conforms to Christ, the whole creation conforms to her in that the whole of creation cooperates for the good of those who love God. Thus the brothers of Christ possess not only the goods of heaven but all the goods of the earth.

---

[59] The translation of Letter 469 is taken from B. James' translation, *The Letters of St. Bernard of Clairvaux* (Chicago: 1953), p. 521. On its authenticity, see D. Farkasfalvy, "The authenticity of Saint Bernard's Letter from His Deathbed," *Analecta Cisterciensia* 36 (1980), pp. 263-268.

The less they desire the things of the earth the more they are the masters of all the earth:

> The faithful man possesses the whole world as his own wealth; he possesses the whole world because both adversity and prosperity, in fact everything equally serves him and cooperates for his good (21 SC 7: I, 126).

Our eschatological consummation is analogous to that of Christ and is caused by Christ. It includes the glorification of our bodies and the deification of our affections (Dil 28: III, 143; 3 OS 3: V, 351). Even if fully purified, the soul is not yet completely free after the death of the body to be totally united with God. The soul's need for her body still keeps her from being absorbed in God. Thus, while the first coming of the Son in the Incarnation intended the redemption of our souls, the goal of his final, glorious coming is the resurrection and glorification of our bodies. Only after receiving our own resurrected and glorified bodies will we become "complete" in ourselves so that nothing which belongs to us will be lacking. Only then can all our affections be fully directed to God.[60]

Until the end of history, there remains another obstacle for the full happiness of the saints: they await the consummation of their number. The transformation of their affections into some kind of divine affection[61] only extends and intensifies their compassion for us who are still struggling here on earth. The saints in heaven cannot feel pain but they feel what we feel when we suffer by taking us into themselves. In all this they act together with their head, the glorified Christ, whose compassion embraces all those who suffer or are in the grip of sin on earth. But at the end of history, with the final separation of the saved and damned and with the glorification of our bodies, there will be no more need for compassion.[62]

---

[60] Dil 29-33: III, 143-147; 2 OS 4-8: V, 345-348.

[61] *"in divinum quendam totus mutatur affectum"* (SC 26:5: I, 173).

[62] Dil 40: III, 153-154; 3 OS 1: V, 349-350; 5 OS 11: V, 369-370; XC 11: IV, 433; 26 SC 5: I, 173.

We will then also completely forget about ourselves and unite our whole selves with the will of God. In this act of becoming one with God's will the whole human being loves God and this love transcends everything human: nothing human remains in the human being so that God may be all in all. In particular, our human affection must "melt away from itself and be poured over into God's will." Our delight will not center on the fulfillment of our needs not even on our own happiness, but on the fact that God's will is fulfilled in us and by us. Then we will love even ourselves for God's sake and everyone and everything else as he loves (Dil 28: III, 143).

> In fact he who adheres to God is one spirit with him and the whole person changes into a somewhat divine affection; being filled with God, he cannot feel or taste anything but God and what God feels and tastes (26 SC 5: I, 173).

It is in this act of loving with our whole selves (*ex tota se*) that we return God's gift of his whole self. It is also in this act of total self-transcendence,[63] that all glorified human beings will perfectly become that one and unique Spouse in whom the Word Bridegroom finds all his delight.

Conclusions:
The Importance of St. Bernard's Christology for Our Age

I hope that this essay provided some evidence to show that Bernard's thought does contain the seeds of a new synthesis between Christology and anthropology for our age.

1. Bernard agrees with our modern sensitivity that sees the human being as a free, self-determining individual. In fact, he points out that free self-determination is the very essence of human nature, and the image of God the Son in us. But Bernard is

---

[63] "*Alioquin quomodo omnia in omnibus erit Deus, si in homine de homine quidquam supererit?*" (Dil 28: III, 143).

no individualist. He shows that individuals can develop themselves only in a twofold process of self-transcendence: by becoming one spirit with Christ and by realizing in themselves the features of the unique Spouse, the Church of Christ.

2. To our contemporaries who prefer to speak about the various forms of self-estrangement rather than sin, Bernard shows that self-alienation and alienation from other people is the result of alienation from God; the latter comes about when we attempt to become what we cannot be: absolute self-possession, our own gods.

3. Bernard views Salvation History as God's work of overcoming this threefold alienation by appealing to the most powerful faculty in us, our ability to love. This divine plan to reorient and develop our capacity to love God, neighbor and the self, and to appreciate everything according to its true value takes into account our fallen nature and designs a strategy to appeal to our freedom. However, this appeal through the events of Jesus' life, death and Resurrection does not remain as it were "outside of us." Through his Spirit, God inspires us within to freely respond to him. However, we may receive God's enabling love only because the Son of God made man has obtained forgiveness for us on the cross from his Father. Thus the way is opened for humankind to full communion with God: the Son offers all of himself (and the whole creation along with himself) to us while asking for a full gift of ourselves to him in love.

Just as the fall of the human race is seen as a threefold alienation, eschatological salvation is celebrated as the overcoming of this alienation in our full unity with God, with ourselves and with our neighbors.

4. Bernard views human misery with a modern sensitivity in that he feels and describes graphically the emotional disorder of fallen humanity. The gradual participation in salvation brings about "a healing of emotions" and at the end a deification of our emotions. This healing takes place to the extent that we participate in the various stages of the self-emptying and the glorification of the Son.

5. Bernard succeeds in laying down the foundations for a universal and Christocentric vision of all history. I don't hesitate to say that Rahner's theory of the anonymous Christian would have

found both a sympathetic hearing and a necessary Christological clarification in an exchange with Bernard. According to Bernard, everyone is offered salvation including even the children of the pagans. But salvation is encountered in the life of the pagans not in the form of accepting or rejecting the fullness of one's human existence but in the form of an implicit faith in Christ the redeemer.

6. In emphasizing the Incarnation as the manifestation of God's humility, Bernard provides the theological context in which the lasting results of the modern "search for the historical Jesus" can find their theological meaning. A truly human Jesus with all the limitations of being a helpless child and a normal human being is for Bernard the most awe-inspiring manifestation of God's self-emptying humility. Bernard shows us that the "low Christology" of modern historical research makes theological sense only as the concrete description of the voluntary humbling himself of the eternal Son of God for our salvation.

7. Bernard's understanding of the appearances of the risen Christ as an adaptation of a transcendent eschatological reality to our sense experience ("*morem gerit nostris sensibus*") points out the way to escape from the impasse of contemporary theology which vacillates between the two extremes of a fundamentalist and a Gnostic interpretation of the appearances. For Bernard Jesus has truly risen in his body but he cannot appear to us as he really is in his glorified, "divinized" state because we are still fleshly beings who can perceive and love only that which is proportionate to our sense experience. The purpose of these "accommodating appearances" is to provide an existential stimulus so that we can liberate ourselves from our clinging to this world and be enabled to develop a spiritual love for the invisible, glorified Lord.

8. Process theology is attractive today because it presents creation, humankind in particular, as an active partner to God. God and humankind are mutually necessary for each other and humankind does contribute to God's evolving perfection. Bernard, on the other hand, makes it very clear that God does not need us, nor do we contribute anything to God's infinite perfection. Nevertheless, the final fruit of redemption is God's *Sponsa*: the bride, virgin and mother who, by sheer grace, is raised in some way to

God's level and becomes a desirable, beautiful partner for God
so that they make each other mutually happy.[64]

9. Today's feminist theology needs Bernard's perspective.
The Word comes to us as a Bridegroom only in the sense that he
is the initiator of the "love affair" and he is the source of the bride's
life and love through the Holy Spirit. But the relationship between
the Word/Bridegroom and the soul/Bride transcends any kind
of sexual love. His transcendence is expressed by a complementary image to the Word Bridegroom in the Word "Wisdom" who
is pictured as feminine.

In the light of the accusations which often label patristic theology as patriarchal and male chauvinist, it is somewhat ironic that
Bernard's theology and the whole patristic and medieval tradition
symbolize all of saved humankind, male and female, by a female
image. Precisely to the extent that humankind comes to its own
perfection as a free and highly desirable partner to God, it is called
Bride, Virgin and Mother.

10. Bernard also provides a neglected perspective for liberation theology. One could hardly find anyone else who saw and criticized from the viewpoint of the Gospel ideal the "systemic" cor-
ruptions of the Church and the society of his age with more passion and theological clear-sightedness than Bernard. Nevertheless,
he is convinced that the victory and dominion of the Christian over
this world is possible even under the most corrupt ecclesial and
political regime. It does not depend on overcoming structural sin
and injustice in Church and society at large but on entering a religious community which models itself on the ideals of the primitive Church: the *vita apostolica*. Once we are conformed through
humility and love to Christ in that community, all of creation conforms to us and recognizes our lordship over the world. For Bernard this means that both successes and failures, favors and per-
secutions, including the injustices of society, sickness and health,
cooperate in serving the good of the Christian. These communities of truly free human beings, the "rulers of creation" will act as
a leaven of justice and renewal for the whole Church which has to

---

[64] "*Cum amat Deus, non aliud vult quam amari: quippe non ad aliud amat, nisi ut
ametur, sciens ipso amore beatos, qui se amaverint*" (83 SC 4: II, 301).

assure that political leaders rule with justice. However, Bernard is more of a realist than to believe that in this world the Church and society will ever reach a utopian state of justice and holiness.

11. For our contemporary obsession with the well-being of our bodies Bernard offers both the shock and comfort of what we may call an eschatological humanism: the role of the body in earthly life is to honor the soul, to help the soul to be reconciled to God and thus regain her own spiritual identity. If the body consumes itself in serving the salvation of the soul in her earthly life, then the body itself will be saved at the end. Just as the desire of the angels was fulfilled by the presence of the glorified body of Christ in heaven, so our desire for the body will be fulfilled at Christ's final coming which will effect the glorification of our bodies. The conformation of our bodies to the glorified body of Christ will be the final consummation of Salvation History. While Bernard is single-mindedly dedicated to restoring (as much as is possible in this world) the freedom of the spirit over the desires of the body, he turns with almost tender affection towards the flesh, offering her the assurance that one day she will be the sole object of Christ's coming in glory and majesty:

> O, if you could only taste this sweetness and appreciate this glory! For I am going to talk about some marvelous realities which are nonetheless true and were never doubted by believers: the Lord of hosts himself, the Lord of power and the King of glory will come down in order to give a new shape to our bodies and conform them to his own body of glory. How great will that glory be, what an unspeakable joy, when the Creator of the universe, who had come beforehand humble and incognito in order to justify our souls, for your glorification, O wretched flesh, will come in a solemn and manifest way, not in weakness, but in his glory and majesty (7 Adv 5: IV, 194).

For the people of our age who are so concerned about the well-being of their bodies in this life and so utterly pessimistic about its fate after death, Bernard's love for the body may serve as a reassuring perspective. His love for the body echoes the love of God who wants to unite even the lowest of his creatures with himself and thus imbue it with divine life and eternal value.

Errata

All the typographical errors printed in *JC* are due to my original typing mistakes:

p. 27, line 7. Instead of "*opthe*" read "*ophthe.*"
p. 77, line 8. Instead of "Mt 3:4" read "Mt 4:4."
p. 98, line 5. Instead of "Mk 14:24" read "Mk 14:25."
p. 131, line 17. Instead of "Lk 24:42-43" read "Lk 23:42-43."
p. 147, line 13. Instead of "20:28-29" read "20:27-28."
p. 159, lines 11 & 29. Instead of "Plato" read "Heraclitus."
p. 189, line 30. The second #62 endnote should be changed to #63 and the text of the endnote should read: "Tr. J.M. Carmody & T.E. Clarke, pp. 39-40."
p. 190, line 27. Instead of endnote #63 read #64 and the text of this endnote should read "Quoted by Athanasius, *Against the Arians*, III, 27."
p. 190, line 31. Delete endnote #64 along with its text.
p. 215, line 21. Instead of "and" read "to."
p. 220, line 29. Instead of "Q 2, 2a 9" read "Q 2, a 9."
p. 221, line 28. Instead of "III, Q 46, 2a 6" read "III, Q 46, a 6."
p. 222, line 10. Instead of "III, Q 48, 2a 6" read "III, Q 48, a 6."
p. 222, line 13. Instead of "III, Q 48, 2a 1-6" read "III, Q 48, a 1-6."
p. 222, line 29. Instead of "III, Q I, 2a 2" read "III, Q 1, a 2."
p. 223, line 7. Instead of "III, Q 48, 2a 3" read "III, Q 48, a 3."
p. 223, line 17. Instead of "III, Q 48, 2a 4-5" read "III, Q 48, a 4-5."
p. 223, line 30. Instead of "III, Q 48, 2a 6" read "III, Q 48, a 6."
p. 224, line 19. Instead of "III, Q 56, 2a 1" read "III, Q 56, a 1."
p. 267, line 26. Instead of "categories?" read "categories."

Endnotes

Part I

#22, line 15. Instead of "*The Second Century* 62 (1987-88)" read "*The Second Century* 6 (1987-88)."

#22, line 22. Instead of "*Elsö ö rész*" read "*Elsö rész.*"

#71, line 1. Instead of "Lk 43,34" read "Lk 24,34."

#81. Delete the mistranslation of the Latin text in lines 79, from "Could you" up to "you define it?"

#170. Add "(New York: Scribner's Son, 1966) pp. 218-262." to "Jeremias, *The Eucharistic Words of Jesus.*"

187, line 6. Instead of "*TWNT2*" read "*TWNT.*"

Part II

#19, line 2. Instead of "*prophorikos*" read "*prosphorikos.*"

#34. Instead of "40:5" read "60:5."

#68. Instead of "*First to Cledonius,* 7" read "*First to Cledonius,* 32."

#71. Instead of "*First to Cledonius,* 4" read "*First to Cledonius,* 20-21."

#104, line 1. Instead of "*CF* 6204.-10" read "*CF* 620 canons 4-10."

#124, line 2. Instead of "*S.T.* III, Q 11, A 10" read "*S.T.* III, Q 2, a 10."

#133. Instead of "vol. 401" read "vol. 40, part 1."

#140. Instead of "vol. 401" read "vol. 40, part 1."

#143, line 1. Instead of "vol. 392" read "vol. 39, part 2."

#167, line 1. Instead of "*CR* 78, 199" read "*Corpus Reformatorum* 78, 199."

#182, line 1. Instead of "*Enzyklopdie*" read "*Enzyklopädie.*"

#255. Add "pp. 50-51; 53" to "Ibid."

Part III

#16, line 1. Instead of "*altkirliche*" read "*altkirchliche.*"

#45, line 2. Instead of "pp. 1181-1185" read "pp. 181-185."

#100, line 15. Instead of "*Theological Investigations,* vol. 16" read "*Theological Investigations,* vol. 12."